BASTA!
Land and the Zapatista Rebellion in Chiapas

For Fran Scher
with wishes for
a happier future
for Mexico and
Chiapas

Best Allen-Cottes

BASTA!
Land and the Zapatista Rebellion in Chiapas

by
George A. Collier
with
Elizabeth Lowery Quaratiello

Foreword by Peter Rosset

A FOOD FIRST BOOK
The Institute for Food and Development Policy
Oakland, California

Library of Congress Cataloging-in-Publication Data:
Collier, George Allen, 1942–
      Basta! : land and the Zapatista rebellion in Chiapas /
George A. Collier, with Elizabeth Lowery Quaratiello ;
foreword by Peter Rosset.
          p.   cm.
      Includes bibliographical references and index.
      ISBN 0-935028-65-X : $12.95
      1. Peasantry — Mexico — Chiapas.   2. Land reform —
Mexico — Chiapas.   3. Agriculture — Economic aspects —
Mexico — Chiapas.   4. Chiapas (Mexico) — Rural
conditions.   5. Chiapas (Mexico) — Economic conditions.
6. Rural development — Mexico — Chiapas.
I. Quaratiello, Elizabeth Lowery, 1964–   II. Title.
HD1531.M6C65   1994
333.3'17275 — dc20   94-36292
                                                              CIP

Printed in the United States of America
10 9 8 7 6 5 4 3 2 1
To order additional copies of this book, please write or call our
distributor:
Subterranean Company
Box 160
265 South Fifth Street
Monroe, Oregon 97456
800-274-7826

Design and typesetting: Harvest Graphics
Cover Design: Lory Poulson
Cover: AP photo © Damian Dovarganes

To David and Lucy

and to Stephen, midnight's child

Contents

Illustrations

Foreword

The Zapatista rebellion that began on January 1st, 1994, was an event laden with significance for Mexico and for the world. Thus this extraordinary book can be read on various levels. First and foremost, it is a clear and informative history of the uprising and its relationship to that most important of commodities in rural areas: land. It shows why indigenous people and peasants in the Mexican state of Chiapas chose to take up arms. Yet it also takes a remarkable step toward a more nuanced understanding of indigenous and peasant communities than we have had before. It helps us understand how and why the Zapatista Army of National Liberation—the EZLN—is different from previous armed struggles in Mesoamerica and elsewhere. Finally, and perhaps most importantly, it is a poignant case study of how neo-liberal economic restructuring—called structural adjustment in the Third World and Reaganomics in the U.S.—reaches into the very heart of communities, enriching the few while impoverishing the many; ultimately turning neighbor against neighbor and leading inexorably toward violent confrontations.

George Collier draws upon 30 years of research among the indigenous people of Chiapas to shatter the images held by the Left and the Right, whether they be of 'noble savages' holding out against the ravages of capitalism or of 'backward Indians' holding back economic development. Taking us inside people's lives, he and Elizabeth Lowery Quaratiello show how the poor in indigenous communities are doubly victimized—first by the relationship between their communities and national or international economies, and second by relatively wealthy leaders inside their own villages who exploit them further in a myriad of ways. Yet Collier and Quaratiello also show how, when given half a chance, peasants and indigenous people can seize upon economic opportunities in dynamic ways that intellectuals of either persuasion had previously claimed were impossible, exposing the myth of the insular community, cut off from the outside world. Without taking this additional step in our understanding of peasant societies, we would be doomed to endlessly repeat the past failures of rural development policies throughout the world.

The rank and file members of the EZLN are refugees from villages where local strongmen, or *caciques,* denied them the right to make a living. Given this anti-leader mentality, it should come as no surprise that Zapatista ideology rejects the vanguardism and top-down organization of previous guerrilla movements. Rather they emphasize communal decision making and stake no claims on state power, instead calling, Gramsci-like, upon Mexican civil society to remake the nation in a form more responsive to the needs of the poor. Collier and Quaratiello show how this uprising, despite coming from largely indigenous communities, reaches out to all of the poor and disenfranchised regardless of their ethnicity, something surprising and perhaps even refreshing in this age of ethnic conflict.

This is a book about the Zapatistas, and about the 'Indigenous' and 'Peasant Questions' that have troubled Latin America for so long. But it is also a book about people's lives, a book that cuts easily across the geographic and cultural distances that separate readers in the North from Mayan communities in Chiapas. It is in showing ordinary lives, complete with petty and not-so-petty struggles, that the authors are at their best. This book makes it absolutely clear what the economic restructuring of the 1980s has left in its wake, and while their chosen case study is of Chiapas, what they have to say is equally relevant to South Central Los Angeles or any other community that has had its fabric ripped asunder by home-grown or exported Reaganomics. The growing gulf between rich and poor leads to the desperation and violence of neighbor against neighbor. In Chiapas, at least, a new social grouping has emerged from the desolation, represented by the Zapatistas and their spokesman, *Sub-comandante Marcos.* Perhaps they are showing all of us a path forward, setting aside the ethnic differences that separate us and the verticalism that often stifles popular movements.

Abbreviations

ANCIEZ	Alianza Nacional Campesina Independiente Emiliano Zapata/National Independent Emiliano Zapata Peasant Alliance
ANAGSA	Aseguradora Nacional Agrícola y Ganadero/National Agriculture and Livestock Insurance Program
ARIC-UU	Asociación Rural de Interés Colectivo - Unión de Uniones/Rural Collective Interest Association - Union of Unions
CCRI	Comité Clandestino de Revolución Indígena/ Committee of Clandestine Indigenous Revolution
CEOIC	Consejo Estatal de Organizaciones Indígenas y Campesinas/Chiapas State Indigenous Peasant Council
CIOAC	Central Independiente de Obreros Agrícolas y Campesinos/Independent Confederation of Agricultural Workers and Peasants
CNC	Confederación Nacional Campesina/National Peasant Confederation
CNPA	Coordinadora Nacional Plan de Ayala/National "Plan de Ayala" Coordinating Committee
CNPI	Consejo Nacional de Pueblos Indígenas/National Council of Indigenous Pueblos
CROM	Confederación Regional Obrera Mexicana/Mexican Regional Labor Confederation
CTM	Confederación de Trabajadores de México/ Confederation of Mexican Workers
EZLN	Ejército Zapatista de Liberación Nacional/Zapatista National Liberation Army
FDN	Frente Democrático Nacional/National Democratic Front
INI	Instituto Nacional Indigenista/National Indianist Institute
INMECAFE	Instituto Mexicano del Café/Mexican Coffee Institute

ISMAM	Indígenas de la Sierra Madre de Motozintla/Indians of the Sierra Madre of Motozintla
LP	Línea Proletaria/Proletarian Line
NAFTA	North American Free Trade Agreement
OCEZ	Organización Campesina Emiliano Zapata/Emiliano Zapata Peasant Organization
ORIACH	Organización Indígena de los Altos de Chiapas/ Indigenous Organization of Highland Chiapas
PAN	Partido Acción Nacional/National Action Party
PP	Política Popular/Popular Politics
PRA	Plan de Rehabilitación Agraria/Agrarian Rehabilitation Plan
PRD	Partido de la Revolución Democrática/Party of the Democratic Revolution
PRI	Partido Revolucionario Institucional/Institutional Revolutionary Party
PRODESCH	Programa de Desarrollo Socioeconómico de los "Altos" de Chiapas/Socioeconomic Development Program for the Highlands of Chiapas
PRONASOL	Programa Nacional de Solidaridad/National Solidarity Program
PST	Partido Socialista de los Trabajadores/Socialist Workers Party
SAM	Sistema Alimentario Mexicano/Mexican Food System
SEDESOL	Secretaría de Desarrollo Social/Ministry of Social Development
SRA	Secretaría de Reforma Agraria/Ministry of Agrarian Reform
UU	Unión de Uniones/Union of Unions

Preface

In January 1991, Zinacanteco Indians in Chiapas questioned me about the Persian Gulf War. Why had Saddam Hussein and George Bush brought countries on opposite sides of the world into war? Would burning Kuwait oil fields truly pollute the world's skies and seas? Might warfare come to Chiapas?

A different kind of war arose in Chiapas on January 1, 1994 when the Zapatista Army of National Liberation (EZLN) rebelled against the Mexican government in a region that seems remote and exotic to many. But Chiapas and the Persian Gulf are closer than one might think, drawn together by the geopolitics of petroleum that have transformed Mexico's agrarian economy since the OPEC crisis stunned the world in 1972.

Mexico began to produce oil for export in the 1970s, pouring borrowed petrodollars into development that drew people out of the countryside and confronted the nation with shortfalls in basic foods and a crisis in agriculture. Subsidies and agrarian reform helped stave off the setbacks in agriculture until 1982, when dropping world oil prices plunged Mexico into a crisis of debt. Austerity and economic restructuring cut support for agrarian programs, and the problems in the countryside worsened. The Zapatista rebellion responded to this crisis.

I began studying peasant agriculture in the highlands of Chiapas in the early 1960s and have witnessed many of the changes that oil-led development has brought to the lives and livelihoods of Zinacantecos and other indigenous peasants of the region. This book about the background to the Zapatista rebellion draws on the unusual privilege of having been able to return to Chiapas repeatedly through more than three decades of dramatic change.

About myself and the perspectives that I bring to this writing, I have the following to say. My values have been shaped by a family firmly committed to New Deal Democratic politics, probably inclining me to sympathy for national states such as Mexico that have embraced responsibilities for popular welfare. Nonetheless, born in 1942, I matured after World War II in the era of Cold War that erased much of our consciousness of class and politics. It was when I began to read about Latin American and Iberian history that I decided to study agrarian politics and change.

At the time of Lázaro Cárdenas's 1934–40 presidency in Mexico, my grandfather, John Collier, Sr., was Commissioner of Indian Affairs in the Roosevelt administration and an activist for Indianism (national programs on behalf of indigenous people) in the Americas. I knew him in his elder years as a somewhat eccentric, introspective, yet visionary person whose love of wilderness and solitude, I later realized, stemmed from how he had come to grips with adolescent depression after the suicide and death of his parents. As an anthropologist, I have always been intrigued by, yet distanced from, Indianism, which I understand in historical perspective as partaking of what Renato Rosaldo describes as "imperialist nostalgia."[1] It is not for lack of interest in the contemporary Maya that I take this position; I have mastered Tzotzil as a way of learning from Zinacanteco and other indigenous people of central highland Chiapas about their history, politics, and views of the world. My experience with and understanding of the Maya contribute to my skepticism of those who interpret the Zapatista movement primarily as a Maya movement when it has so much in common with the shared concerns of the class of rural poor. Indigenous people who have responded to the Zapatista calling have done so primarily because they see justice in the Zapatista's political and economic demands on behalf of the countryside's poor.

I am also wary of idealizations of peasants. I see today's peasantries as less egalitarian and more differentiated by class and politics than do many analysts. The appeal to collective sentiments is often combined with maneuvering for personal power. Many of the Mexican indigenous and other peasants I shall talk about have protagonized activism for land, or have challenged the ruling party on behalf of their fellows at one stage of their political careers while taking the side of the national state and exercising its power at another stage. Their rise to power and their exercise of power have as much to do with the relationships in which peasants strive for advantage over one another as with the ways in which the regional or national bourgeoisie gain advantage over them.

I have learned a great deal about Chiapas from the work and insight of colleagues in what began as the Harvard Chiapas Project, led by Evon Z. Vogt, who introduced me and dozens of other students to research in highland Chiapas. Frank and Francesca Cancian, Jane Collier, John Haviland, Robert and Mimi Laughlin, Jan and Diane Rus, and Evon and Catherine Vogt have shared lives and work in more ways than I can credit.

Robert Alvarez, Merielle Flood, Daniel Mountjoy, and Ronald Nigh have collaborated in some of my research and writing. Ramón González Ponciano, Aída Hernández Castillo, Gary Gossen, Lourdes de León, June Nash, and Stuart Plattner have generously shared writing and advice. I am grateful for the research assistance of Namino Glantz, José Hernández Pérez, María Hernández Pérez, Antonio Pérez Hernández, and Apen Ruiz and for the hospitality of Marcy Jacobsen, Janet Marren and Kippy Nigh. This book has also benefitted from comments and suggestions from Federico Besserer, Frank Cancian, Jane Collier, Mimi Laughlin, Bill Maurer, Stuart and Phyllis Plattner, Lucía Rayas, and Peter Rosset; and from research material made available by James Breedlove, Dan Rozkuszka, and Teresa Sierra. I also wish to thank staff, student, and faculty colleagues at the Department of Anthropology, Stanford, for opportunities to talk about my analysis of the events in Chiapas.

I am very grateful for the assistance of institutions and colleagues in Chiapas. The Instituto Chiapaneco de Cultura (ICC) has generously shared publications of vital research by scholars of the region. I especially appreciate the assistance extended to me by Andrés Fábregas Puig, Director General of the ICC, and by Jesús Morales Bermúdez. I thank the Centro de Estudios Universitarios (CEU) and librarian María Elena Fernández Galán for published and unpublished source materials. The Centro de Investigaciones Ecológicas del Sureste (CIES) has shared library and map resources, and I thank Pablo Farías, Ignacio March, and Manuel Parra for their collegiality and assistance. CIESAS, Sureste, the regional office of Mexico's Centro de Investigaciones y Estudios Superiores en Antropología Social, has also shared library materials, as has INAREMAC, the Instituto de Asesoría Antropológica para la Región Maya, A.C. I appreciate access to the map collections of Na Bolom and of the Fundación Arqueológica Nuevo Mundo in San Cristóbal de las Casas.

To the people of Zinacantán, and especially to those of the hamlet of Apas, I owe special thanks for having been welcomed over the years as a guest and researcher.

I am grateful for research support from the National Science Foundation for the study of "Agrarian Change in Southeastern Mexico" (BNS-8804607) and for "Methodological Training for a GIS Application in Cultural Anthropology" (DBS-9221376); from the Consortium of International Earth Sciences Information Network (CIESIN) for study of "Deforestation, Land Use & Development in the Greater Mayan Region"; from the Stanford Humanities Center for time to think and write about the changing livelihoods and politics of Zinacantán; and from the Center for Latin American Studies for research support in Chiapas during summer 1993.

The publishers of *BioScience, Cultural Survival Quarterly, Mexican Studies/Estudios Mexicanos,* and *Research in Economic Anthropology* graciously allowed me to draw upon maps and materials in my previously published work. Chapter Five draws extensively on an essay published as a discussion paper by the United Nations Research Institute for Social Development. Chapter Six is based on a recent article I wrote for *Dialectical Anthropology* (Kluwer Academic Publishers). I am grateful for permission to borrow from these previous works.

Elizabeth Quaratiello and I have collaborated in writing this book, which is based on my research and other scholarly writing. We wish to thank our families for patience and forbearance in allowing us to bring the work to fruition.

George A. Collier
Stanford, California

Introduction

When a housemaid in the Chiapas state capital, Tuxtla Gutiérrez, suddenly quit her job, why had she just used her entire Christmas bonus to buy hundreds of bandages?

Why did a man purchase an itinerant merchant's entire stock of rubber boots in March 1993 at the entrance to Palenque, Chiapas's famous classic Mayan ruin?

What made peasants eking out a precarious existence in the rain forests of eastern Chiapas cite "war" as a threat more dangerous to the world than "poverty," "disease," "deforestation," or "pollution" in a 1992 survey of attitudes about global change?[1]

In the summer of 1993, Tucson writer Leslie Marmon Silko's *Almanac of the Dead*, a novel prognosing native American rebellion from Chiapas to Arizona, suddenly captured an audience of readers in Chiapas. Was there a special reason for such fascination?

The answers to many such puzzles suggested themselves on January 1, 1994, when the EZLN (the *Ejército Zapatista de Liberación Nacional* or Zapatista Army of National Liberation), equipped with rubber boots, homemade army uniforms, bandanas, ski masks, and weapons ranging from handmade wooden rifles to Uzi machine guns, seized towns in eastern and central Chiapas, proclaiming a revolution on the inaugural day of the North American Free Trade Agreement (NAFTA).

Taking advantage of the New Year holiday to catch security forces off guard, the Zapatistas—a force of young, disciplined and mostly indigenous men and women soldiers—ransacked the town halls of Altamirano, Chanal, Huistán, Las Margaritas, Oxchuc, Ocosingo, and San Cristóbal de las Casas—once the colonial seat of government of Chiapas and today an important commercial and tourist center. Some burned district attorney, judicial, and police records (but spared archives in San Cristóbal that a local scholar told them had historic value). Others fanned out into the

1

mountains to seek recruits from among the indigenous and other peasants of the region.

Treating startled tourists and civilians with courtesy, the EZLN pronounced itself in rebellion against the government, the army, and the police. In printed circulars and broadcasts from captured Ocosingo radio station XOECH, the Zapatistas declared:

> **Hoy Decimos Basta! Today we say enough is enough! To the people of Mexico: Mexican brothers and sisters:** We are a product of 500 years of struggle: first against slavery, then during the War of Independence against Spain led by insurgents, then to promulgate our constitution and expel the French empire from our soil, and later [when] the dictatorship of Porfirio Díaz denied us the just application of the Reform laws and the people rebelled and leaders like Villa and Zapata emerged, poor men just like us. We have been denied the most elemental education so that others can use us as cannon fodder and pillage the wealth of our country. They don't care that we have nothing, absolutely nothing, not even a roof over our heads, no land, no work, no health care, no food, and no education. Nor are we able freely and democratically to elect our political representatives, nor is there independence from foreigners, nor is there peace nor justice for ourselves and our children.[2]

Invoking Article 39 of Mexico's 1917 Constitution, which invests national sovereignty and the right to modify government in the people of Mexico, they called on other Mexicans to help them depose the "illegal dictatorship" of President Carlos Salinas de Gortari's government and party. They declared war on the Mexican armed forces and called on international organizations and the Red Cross to monitor under the Geneva Conventions of War. They appealed to other Mexicans to join their insurgency.

Within twenty-four hours, the EZLN launched an attack on the Rancho Nuevo army base about six miles southeast of San Cristóbal and freed 179 prisoners from a nearby penitentiary. They kidnapped Absalón Castellanos Domínguez, governor of Chiapas from 1982 to 1988, announcing he would be tried summarily and shot for crimes of repression. Instead, he was "sentenced" to a life term of hard peasant labor.

The Mexican government quickly moved 12,000 troops and equipment into the region. Within days, and after two pitched battles, the Zapatistas retreated east and southward out of the

Figure 0.1 **Chiapas and the Area of Zapatista Rebellion.**

Chiapas central highlands into rugged and inaccessible strong-
holds in the tropical forests of the eastern lowlands. Backed by air
strikes, federal troops pursued the EZLN in armored vehicles to
where roads give way to wilderness.

By that time, journalists from around the world had arrived on
the scene to chronicle the Zapatista's exploits and explore their
motives, which struck chords of sympathy with the Mexican public. Reporters portrayed the rebels as Maya Indians upset over
years of poverty and discrimination as they began to write
poignant articles describing the abuses heaped upon the Indians of
Mexico's southernmost state. Human rights organizations that
had for some time been trying to alert the world to the plight of
the region's poor suddenly found an avid audience as they began
to document federal army abuses against Zapatista prisoners and
civilians caught up in the warfare.

The rebels, disguised with bandanas and ski masks, became
instant icons, their images replicated on everything from cloth
dolls sold in Mexico's outdoor marketplaces to cartoons in Mexico
City's daily newspapers. Zapatista images even appeared on con-
dom wrappers. Guessing the identity of "Sub-Comandante
Marcos," the shadowy, green-eyed ideologue and military director
of the uprising, suddenly became a popular obsession.

The Mexican government sought at first to paint the Zapatista
rank and file as guileless but gullible natives inspired and led by
foreign subversives. But public opinion, international scrutiny, and
widespread dissension within the ranks of the ruling party itself
soon led Salinas de Gortari to acknowledge that the Zapatistas had
justifiable grievances based on Chiapas's and Mexico's internal
affairs. Salinas fired Interior Minister José Patroncinio González
Garrido, who as governor of Chiapas from 1988 to 1993 had been
accused of repression and abuses against peasants. The President
then declared a unilateral cease-fire on January 12, calling on the
Zapatistas to lay down their arms and negotiate with a specially
designated Commission for Peace and Reconciliation.

In the weeks that followed, tensions rose. Citizens seized dozens
of town halls in Chiapas and neighboring states to protest that
incumbent mayors, most of whom were pawns of the governing
party, had stolen office through fraudulent elections. In eastern
Chiapas, peasants invaded private ranches. Some landowners fled,

others counterattacked with hired gunmen. A broad coalition of peasant and indigenous organizations denounced the government for past neglect and abuse and proclaimed themselves in favor of Zapatista demands for reforms.

Peace talks finally began on February 21 in San Cristóbal de las Casas, under the aegis of the Catholic diocese and noted liberation theologian Bishop Samuel Ruiz García. Salinas designated Manuel Camacho Solís as the government's negotiator, a man respected for the integrity and negotiating skills he had demonstrated as former mayor of Mexico City and as foreign affairs minister. As a gesture of good will, the Zapatistas released hostage and former governor Absalón Castellanos Domínguez. With Sub-Comandante Marcos as their public relations and military spokesperson, the EZLN's general command, the Committee of Clandestine Indigenous Revolution, made up of eighteen representatives of four Mayan-language ethnic groups, began the talks and demanded attention to thirty-four broad-ranging issues of political, economic, and social reform. Two weeks later, negotiators announced thirty-two tentative accords, and the talks recessed to allow both sides to consult with their constituencies. Mexicans breathed a sigh of relief and hope.

Their optimism proved ephemeral. The uprising had thrown Mexico into crisis, calling into question President Salinas de Gortari's program to restructure and modernize the Mexican economy. Deep fissures in the Mexican political system, papered over during Salinas's regime by a facade of "consensus" building, had revealed themselves to international scrutiny as the highly publicized rebellion evoked public debate over government fraud, corruption, and dereliction of duty to Mexico's peasant and indigenous poor. It became apparent that the government had known about the guerrilla army in Chiapas for over a year. Rumors flew that Salinas had done nothing for fear of jeopardizing U.S. congressional approval of NAFTA, or that hard-liners in the ruling party and in the military had lent support to the rebels in protest against Salinas's policies.

The presidential candidacy of Salinas's hand-picked successor, Luis Donaldo Colosio Murrieta, seemed in jeopardy as speculation flared that Salinas might replace Colosio with peace negotiator Camacho, or that Camacho, whom Salinas had initially passed over in favor of Colosio, might declare a renegade candidacy. For the first time in more than half a century, it began to seem as though Mexico's ruling party, the Institutional Revolutionary Party (PRI), might actually have to relinquish power in the presidential elections slated for August 21, 1994.

On March 22, Camacho declared that he would not run for President, but the next day PRI presidential candidate Luis Donaldo Colosio fell to an assassin's bullet, shocking the nation and provoking charges that the killing had been plotted within the PRI itself.

The violence polarized public debates over the Zapatistas and the government. Although the PRI hastily replaced Colosio with Ernesto Zedillo Ponce de León in the hopes of capitalizing on the reaction against violence, Zedillo, a Yale-trained economist who had been Colosio's election advisor, ran a lackluster campaign. But so did candidates of the opposition parties, Cuauhtémoc Cárdenas of the Party of the Democratic Revolution (PRD) and Diego Fernández de Cevallos of the National Action Party (PAN).

Then, on June 12, the Zapatista rank and file rejected the tentative peace accord their own representatives had negotiated with the government, calling for a national convention to revamp the political system while refusing to lay down their arms. Zedillo deemed the earlier negotiations with the EZLN a failure, blaming Camacho, who then resigned as the government's peace negotiator. As leading Mexicans began to suggest publicly that Mexico might become ungovernable, regardless of the outcome of the August elections, Mexico's Jorge Carpizo MacGregor, a jurist and former human rights commissioner who had agreed in January to step in as interior minister to oversee the elections, submitted his resignation, asserting that an unnamed party was making fair elections impossible. Salinas persuaded Carpizo to withdraw his resignation, but uncertainties continued to grow as the Zapatistas called for a convention prior to the elections to rewrite Mexico's Constitution.

This is a book about the background to the fateful Zapatista rebellion. Despite widespread fascination with the uprising, little is understood about its root causes. I want to look behind the romantic images, instant analyses,[3] and outrage prompted by the rebellion, to explore the circumstances and forces—both domestic and international—that created a situation ripe for rebellion.

The region behind the headlines is a complicated one. Chiapas is sometimes described as a picturesque backwater—a quaint stop on the tourist circuit where time has stood still and Maya Indians can be observed performing their age-old crafts and rituals. But beneath the surface seen by the casual visitor, Chiapas is filled with paradoxes that defy easy categorization. In addition to peasants who weave and wear the traditional *huipul* (tunic) and carry loads on *tumplines*, there are peasants who dress in jeans and drive trucks. Within even the tiniest Indian hamlets there are wealthy entrepreneurs who own such modern luxury items as televisions and videocassette recorders; poor, marginalized farm workers; and opportunistic political bosses. The state has plenty of wealthy *ladinos* (nonindigenous Mexicans of the region) who sympathize with the Zapatistas and poor peasants who do not. There are disaffected intellectuals, grassroots organizers, elite colonial families, and ranchers, each with their own political agenda. And in this place where Catholics and Protestants have clashed bitterly, where women are praised for passivity rather than activism, a nonsectarian rebellion has arisen, and mothers, wives and daughters are among those who make up the ranks of the Zapatista army.

What is it that unites those who took up arms with the Zapatistas? In contrast to some analysts, I posit that it is primarily a peasant rebellion, not an exclusively Indian rebellion, because although the Zapatistas are demanding rights for indigenous peoples, they are first and foremost calling attention to the plight of Mexico's rural poor and peasants, both indigenous and nonindigenous. By *peasants*, I mean rural people who produce their own food or who are closely connected to others who produce for subsistence, as contrasted with those who farm commercial crops primarily for sale and profit. In southern Mexico, many peasants, but not all, are *indigenous* people, descendants of those who were conquered and subordinated by the Spanish during the period of colonial rule.[4]

Some may wonder why the rebellion was instigated by peasants and not by the urban poor or those who toil in the *maquiladoras*, people who have certainly suffered greatly in recent years. Although there is no clear answer to this question, one possible explanation is that on top of the severe hardships peasants have had to endure during the past decade of economic restructuring, they were also disappointed by a number of broken promises from the government: land reform that never occurred; price supports guaranteed, then taken away; and credits extended, then withdrawn. When, in 1992, the government of President Salinas de Gortari brought land reform—the issue on which his party had originally risen to power—to a halt, he signalled an abrupt end to a traditional government covenant with the peasantry and deprived many peasants not just of the possibility of improving their livelihoods, but of their power as a constituency. The Zapatistas are trying to reclaim that constituency.

The Zapatista rebellion bears some resemblance to the revolutionary movements of Central America, in that those movements also involved peasants who had no safety net to help cope with marginalization. Mexico's government, however, has been much more stable than any of Central America's regimes and has steadfastly—and successfully—fought off involvement in the geo-politics of the Cold War.[5] Until the 1982 debt crisis, Mexico also catered to peasants as a distinct constituency—something most Central American governments never even pretended to do. One of the paradoxes of the rebellion is that the Zapatistas have responded to the adversity of eastern Chiapas more as Mexican nationals than as doctrinaire revolutionaries. While they are demanding changes for their region and for the rural poor in other areas, they are also holding Mexico's ruling party responsible for undemocratic politics and for betraying historic commitments to social welfare when it opened Mexico up to free trade and foreign investment.

As economic and political forces have transformed peasant farming, peasant communities have become less egalitarian, demarcated by class and by national political affiliation. My observations are drawn from research I performed as an anthropologist during three decades spent studying agrarian change in highland Chiapas, including ways in which Mexico's oil boom of the 1970s and the resulting debt crisis of the 1980s redefined the lives and roles of the region's peasants. Among the indigenous peasants I know, I saw a gap grow ever wider between the wealthy, who were able to infuse their farming with cash derived from wage work near oil fields, on dam projects, and in urban construction projects, and the poor, who are finding it increasingly impossible to be able to afford to farm even their own land.

Some peasants in Chiapas have been able to weather the changes wrought by Mexico's economic restructuring by diversifying their farming activities, becoming produce and flower merchants, or starting up transport businesses. But many have not. Their successes and failures have often resulted from and contributed to politics, as I will show by tracing the rise of local political bosses who have used their ties with the Institutional Revolutionary Party (PRI) to establish monopolies on small businesses and quell opposition in their towns. Economic restructuring brought particular suffering to the inhabitants of the eastern part of Chiapas, from which the rebels draw the majority of their members, and where cultural isolation, political exclusion, and economic depression have combined to leave people in what is commonly called Mexico's "last frontier" without hope and without even the most basic necessities of life.

Because the situation of peasants in Mexico's countryside seems so bleak, the Zapatista rebellion inspired enormous sympathy from people throughout the world who read about the uprising in their newspapers and watched reports about it on television. Journalists tended to paint an image of the poor, honest peasants on one side and the greedy ranchers and corrupt politicians on the other.

This idealization of peasants is inaccurate, however, because some of the inequalities in the countryside are the result of stratification within peasant communities, not merely the result of injustices heaped upon them from outside. Understanding indigenous politics in this way necessarily complicates the sympathies one might hold toward peasants, but I view this as salutary. I think we misrepresent peasants if we allow ourselves to view them in simplistic terms—as either the passive victims of the state or as "noble savages" who can reinvigorate modern society with egalitarian and collective values. By acknowledging tensions and differences in peasant communities, we face up to both the virtue and the vice inherent in peasants' exercise of power over one another, and we integrate individual agency into our understanding of peasant communities. We also arrive at an appreciation of why not all peasant and indigenous groups welcomed the Zapatistas. In some highland communities, some people referred to the Zapatistas in native Tzotzil as "trouble makers" or as "thieves"— a reference to marauders who roamed the countryside in the

1910–20 decade of the Mexican Revolution. Others told me that when the Zapatistas fanned into the mountains to look for recruits, a giant snake and a whirlwind—ancestor deities—rose in their paths to block off the entrances to Zinacantán and Chamula, communities whose leaders are loyal to the PRI.

The Zapatista uprising has forced a public debate about Mexico's priorities and has galvanized many impoverished Mexicans to demand better lives, even as it has to some extent polarized relations among indigenous peoples' organizations in Chiapas.

Synopsis

This book begins with a broad overview of the social, political, economic, and ethnic history of Chiapas from colonial times to the present day. We trace the development of the state from a logging and coffee-growing center in the nineteenth century to the integral role it plays in Mexico today, providing the country with half of its hydroelectric power and much of its oil, as well as many basic foods such as corn and beans. We look at the bitter history of the indigenous people and their subjugation under the Spanish *conquistadores*, a legacy of injustice that continues to taint present day relations between indigenous and non-indigenous Mexicans. We look at land distribution and the various means used to effect it during the past century, providing a background against which the current political agitation can be viewed.

Turning to the eastern Chiapas heartland of the Zapatista uprising, Chapter 2 explores peasant life in this remote tropical wilderness that has become famous as the "jungle headquarters" of the EZLN. Virtually unpeopled until the middle of this century, eastern Chiapas has been settled by waves of peasants fleeing land scarcity and religious persecution in the highlands as well as by peasants from other states in Mexico. We chronicle the constant struggle of these settlers who have had to compete with loggers, ranchers, and one another for land and livelihood as deforestation and soil erosion continue to claim more and more of the rain forest. Eastern Chiapas in many ways exemplifies the marginalization of the poorest peasants in contemporary Mexico—it is a region completely cut off from government services, political power and economic opportunity. Without roads, cities or even small towns, eastern Chiapas is a kind of dumping ground for the marginalized, in which all of the hardships peasants confront in the highlands are exacerbated. This chapter explores the role that such circumstances played in fueling the frustrations on which the Zapatistas capitalized.

Chapter 3 traces the social history of eastern Chiapas, focusing on the cultural and religious factors that may have helped to create a climate in which radical politics were more readily accepted than in other areas of Mexico. We look at the growth of grassroots peasant organizations, study their successes and failures, and investigate the ways in which macroeconomic events—such as the collapse of coffee prices in 1989—affected the everyday lives of small farmers in eastern Chiapas. This chapter describes the milieu in which the EZLN grew and gained momentum.

Chapter 4 takes a more in-depth look at the effect of macroeconomic trends on peasant life. We review the development of Mexico's energy economy and examine in detail the negative effects it had on the southern part of the country and the nation as a whole as resources were shifted away from agriculture. In particular, we look at how the oil boom affected peasant migration and delve into the debates that arose over whether Mexico, flooded with cheap corn from Kansas, needed or could even afford peasants any more. We discuss the events that led up to the 1982 debt crisis and examine the aftermath of the austerity program Mexico was pressured to undertake by the international banking community, paying close attention to the revision of the country's agrarian subsidy system and the ways in which peasants responded to the changes. We take up the theme of peasant-initiated economic restructuring, and the diversification of peasant economic activities during the oil boom. This restructuring is little known to scholars and policy makers, in part because their analytical frameworks do not embrace the scope of the far-flung enterprises, such as flower retailing, with which many peasants are experimenting, often in new cooperative associations.

Chapter 5 looks within communities to explore who profits and who loses from restructuring. We examine how economic distinctions have changed the relationships among women and men, young and old, and within communities. The widening gap between rich and poor has broken down many of the relationships of mutual dependency that once helped poorer citizens, and leaders within communities have begun to shuck off their responsibilities to their poorer constituents.

Chapter 6 explores the subtle and not so subtle ways that dissidents are dealt with in the Indian hamlets of Chiapas. We look at how political leaders undermine opponents' recourse to customary law while restricting their access to public funds. We look at the recent phenomenon of expelling dissident "Protestants" from Catholic villages, often for political reasons—an unconstitutional practice, which the government nonetheless tolerates as consistent with native rights to self determination, a justification that masks the political expedience of supporting indigenous henchmen at the local level. We examine the government's Solidarity Program, which was ostensibly designed to alleviate poverty, but which instead became an instrument for rewarding political loyalty and contributed to the anger and frustration expressed through the Zapatista rebellion.

The final chapter explores the implication of the rebellion for Mexico's political future and contains some policy recommendations for how Mexico might capitalize constructively on peasants' demonstrable capacity to embrace and effect change. We look at the organization of the EZLN, examine what politicians might learn from them, and ponder the efficacy of impoverishing huge numbers of people in order to achieve a "modern" economy.

In writing about the causes of the rebellion, I want to raise questions about the social and economic costs of restructuring and suggest that the contributions of small-scale agriculturalists need to be considered when evaluating policies for a nation's fiscal health. Because peasant families often produce only enough food for their own consumption, the product of subsistence farming is not given a value in traditional models of economic analysis. Subsistence crops are neither bought nor sold and are thus often overlooked in calculations of the gross domestic product or income. When economists deride small scale peasant agriculture in Mexico as inefficient and call for its replacement with large-scale agribusinesses, they ignore the fact that such "modern" enterprises often displace as many people as they employ, upsetting the delicate balance between subsistence and marginalization in rural Mexico. Moreover, even those analyses that do focus on small-scale agriculture tend to miss the ways that peasants have restructured their own productive capacity through new micro enterprises. In Chiapas, such restructuring has not been acknowledged by politicians and development planners for the potential benefits peasants themselves can contribute to the revitalization of the Mexican economy, if they are supported rather than shunned.

I. CHIAPAS AND MEXICO

The Zapatista uprising caught both Mexicans and Mexico watchers by surprise. Chiapas seemed an unlikely place for a revolution to start. Chiapas peasants have been among the most reliable supporters of the ruling party since the 1930s, and the peasants who took up arms in January were from the most isolated part of the country. Could their demands for political and economic changes on a national level be taken seriously? When the government made overtures to the EZLN as merely a "political force in formation," Sub-Comandante Marcos angrily retorted that the indigenous people of Chiapas had been exploited for centuries and had every right to make demands of the Mexican political and economic system:

> Why does the government [refuse to put] national politics on the agenda for negotiation? Are the indigenous people of Chiapas "Mexicans" only for the purpose of being exploited? Do they have no right to speak out on national politics? Does the nation claim Chiapas's petroleum, its electric power, its raw materials, its labor—in effect all of Chiapas's life blood—*except indigenous Chiapanecans' opinion* regarding the country's future? What sort of citizens does the government take indigenous Chiapanecans to be? Are they "citizens in formation?" Does the government still treat them as little children, as "adults in formation?"[1]

In light of the region's poverty, racism and history of exploitation, why hadn't peasants taken up arms long ago? We shall see that in centuries past Chiapas's Indians *did* rebel against oppression and exploitation. But because of land reform after the Revolution they came to see the government as an ally—until the Salinas government brought agrarian reform to a halt.

While its ancient Mayan ruins, colonial towns, and colorful culture have attracted a steady stream of scholars and adventurers, for the most part Chiapas has been little known and visited by the rest of the world. Its mountains, cloud forests, canyons, and jungles are not easily accessible to tourists, and its major cities, small by Mexican standards, rise at the end of long, winding roads. But outsiders have nonetheless exploited its natural resources. The Spanish arrived in the sixteenth century, seeking riches, and were followed by Europeans and North Americans in the nineteenth century who coveted Chiapas's precious mahogany and coffee. Today, Chiapas is almost an internal colony for the rest of Mexico, providing oil, electricity, timber, cattle, corn, sugar, coffee, and beans, but receiving very little in return. Chiapas is aptly described as "a rich land, a poor people."[2]

Chiapas has the highest concentration of indigenous people in Mexico and is one of the country's poorest states. Most of Chiapas's wealth is concentrated in the hands of the small number of *ladino* ranching families who have dominated Chiapas politics for two centuries. A rise in interest in indigenous peoples has helped to create some tourism and a market for native handicrafts, but endemic racism continues to mar relations between Indians and nonindigenous Mexicans.

Chiapas lags behind the rest of Mexico in almost every way measurable: household income, education, and basic standard of living fall far behind the national average, and infant mortality is much higher. Many indigenous people in Chiapas are illiterate and only about half of the men and a tiny percentage of the women speak Spanish. According to census figures, only 11 percent of adults earn what the government calls moderate incomes of at least $3,450 per year (vs. 24 percent nationally); less than 50 percent of households have running water (vs. 67 percent nationally); and only 14 percent have televisions (vs. 45 percent nationally). It is important to note that most of the development money that has been funnelled into Chiapas has been used to build infrastructure such as roads and dams that will help transport products from the state to the rest of Mexico.[3]

With only 3 percent of the nation's population, Chiapas produced an astounding 13 percent of the country's corn and 54 percent of Mexico's hydroelectric power. It also produced 5 percent of the country's timber, 4 percent of its beans, 13 percent of its gas and 4 percent of its oil. Ironically, nearly half of Chiapas is without electricity, including most of the regions peopled by Indians (see Figure 1.1).[4]

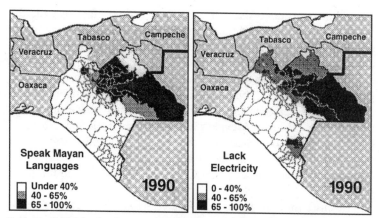

Figure 1.1 "A Rich Land, a Poor People." Chiapas produces much of Mexico's hydroelectric power, yet many areas populated by indigenous people remain without electricity or other basic services.

In addition to food and electricity, Chiapas has for many years supplied Mexico with another vitally important, albeit hard to quantify, resource: political support. Although it is impossible to assess the true numbers involved because of widespread election fraud, the Institutional Revolutionary Party (PRI) has always claimed victory on the basis of overwhelming support from Mexico's rural south. In the 1988 presidential elections, which opposition parties vigorously and effectively contested in northern and metropolitan Mexico, 89.9 percent of Chiapas voters, including impoverished Indian peasants, allegedly turned out for the PRI.

To understand Chiapas's rebellion, we must explore why so stable a regime has been challenged by some of its ostensibly strongest supporters. This chapter looks at Chiapas's relationship to Mexico and examines how it came to pass that the national government was able to tap Chiapas's resources and loyalties so effectively, especially in the central and western parts of the state.

The Legacy of Conquest

The first town the Zapatistas seized was San Cristóbal de las Casas, a small city surrounded by pine forests in the mountainous highlands of central Chiapas. Once the colonial capital of the region, the city retains many vestiges of its colonial past. Baroque churches stand over Indian markets and some neighborhoods continue to produce the same goods they manufactured for the Spanish crown. Some of San Cristóbal's elite families pride themselves on being able to trace their ancestry back to the conquistadors who established the city as Ciudad Real in the 1530s; others emphasize the city's association with Bartolomé de las Casas, "the Protector of Indians," who, as Bishop of Chiapas in the sixteenth century, excoriated the conquistadors for their abuse of indigenous peoples. Prior to Mexico's independence from Spain in 1821, Chiapas was governed by the colonial administration of Guatemala, but when Chiapas became part of Mexico in 1824, Ciudad Real was renamed San Cristóbal de las Casas in honor of the bishop.

The city's modern Hotel de Mazariegos, which became a headquarter for journalists following the rebellion, is named after the city's 1528 founder, conquistador Diego de Mazariegos. Until recently, a bronze statue of de Mazariegos, sword in hand, dominated the courtyard of the beautiful baroque Santo Domingo church and monastery where de las Casas once preached. On October 12, 1992, the Christopher Columbus quincentennial, several hundred Indians marched into San Cristóbal in what may have been a precursor to the Zapatista rebellion. They tore down Diego de Mazariegos's statue, bound it in ropes, and dragged it through the streets of the city as conquistadors once did to punish rebellious Indian subjects.

Chiapas was not easily or quickly conquered by the Spanish. During the 1520s, conquistadors and their native allies from central Mexico launched expeditions into the area. But the region was not completely brought under Spanish dominion until Diego de Mazariegos invaded the highlands, which was peopled with natives who had their own distinct languages and cultures. To the north and east of Ciudad Real, indigenous peoples spoke languages of the Mayan family: Tzotzil, Tzeltal, Chol, Tojolabal. Those to the west and south, especially in the Grijalva River valley, spoke Zoque, the language of the Chiapanec kingdom centered in Chiapa de Corzo.

Subdued by conquest, Indians were forced to help build Ciudad Real, which became the seat of the colonial administration and the base of the Dominicans and other Catholic friars in Chiapas. Ciudad Real also became home to a growing *mestizo* (mixeddescent) population of artisans and tradespeople. The Spanish established ranches in the temperate foothills ringing the highlands and introduced cattle, wheat, pigs, chickens, sugar and countless other products of Iberian heritage. Indians labored on these ranches as part of the tribute they owed their conquerors, who also demanded tribute goods of cloth and dyes. The colonial overlords resettled some Indians to the highlands as a ready source of labor for the authorities in Ciudad Real. They also conscripted Indians to work on ranches and plantations in the lowlands.[5]

While colonial society thrived in the highlands, it disintegrated in the lowlands, which were largely deforested, and alternately humid or torrid by season. Disease and exploitation decimated the native population, who were unable to ward off the Old World diseases of the conquistadors, such as smallpox and measles, or the yellow fever and malaria introduced by African slaves. Entire settlements died out, such as that of Copanaguastla, on the edge of the Grijalva River valley, where Dominican friars had converted Indians to Catholicism and then put them to work cultivating cotton and sugar.[6]

As the indigenous people died—and the Spanish faced a declining labor pool—colonial authorities brought their enterprises in the lowlands to a halt and concentrated on settling natives in the temperate highlands surrounding Ciudad Real, where the milder climate also favored Iberian crops and livestock. In eastern Chiapas, the Spanish organized expeditions to hunt down Chol-speaking Lacandón Indians and resettle them to the north and west foothills, where they could serve the labor needs of colonial ranchers. Eastern Chiapas came to be known as a depeopled or deserted area.[7]

By the seventeenth and eighteenth centuries, the colonial authorities had organized Indian townships around Ciudad Real to produce certain products. Each town fulfilled its tribute obligation to the Crown by specializing in a product or trade, for example curing hides, making pottery, weaving cloth, or growing tobacco, cochineal, or cacao. Several towns delivered cotton to colonial authorities to pass on to other towns to spin into thread, which was transferred to others to weave into the cloth that authorities sold or traded. The Spanish got rich on the tribute goods and labor of Indians. In addition to the materials mentioned above, indigo and cochineal were shipped to Spain as treasured dyes to compete with the royal purple and red dyegoods that the Florentines had monopolized.[8]

The economic specialization of the Indian townships probably contributed to the collective identities that have come to be associated with them. Each town organized ceremonial life and public expenditures as a corporation under the direction of its native nobility and established public celebrations and civic organizations that continue to distinguish indigenous towns today. Prohibited by dress codes that restricted the Indian use of Spanish clothing, each township developed its own style of weaving and embroidery— styles still reflected in ethnic costumes that distinguish highland Indian townships today.

San Cristóbal also retains vestiges of its colonial economic organization. When I first visited the city in 1960, artisanal production was, in large part, still associated with the ladino *barrios*, as it had been in colonial times. Each barrio had its own church and the barrio guilds that were once the center of their neighborhoods' economic and ceremonial life. San Antonio was the barrio of the *coheteros*, who manufactured skyrockets, fireworks, and gunpowder. Leatherworking was concentrated along the Calle Real de Guadalupe and candlemaking in the barrio of the Merced (whose church was established by the Mercedarian order). The Cerrillo district still specializes in carpentry—much of it undertaken with tools developed by woodworkers of the Renaissance, as illustrated in the notebooks of Leonardo da Vinci. Indigo dye vats are still worked in the Mexicanos barrio, which was originally settled by allies of the Spanish conquistadors from central Mexico. *Cuxtitaleros*, residents of the city's easternmost ward, specialized in long-distance trade with the remote ranches on the fringes of the highlands. In colonial times, the Spanish and mestizo residents of Ciudad Real also worked as butchers, tailors, blacksmiths, tinsmiths, shoemakers, bakers, potters, goldsmiths, and cigarmakers. Women made clothing and cigarettes as specialties and the town had a hefty complement of lawyers and administrators. Much of this economy, however, relied on the raw materials, food, and fuel obtained from the native hinterlands.

Throughout the colonial period, the Spanish governed Indians as subordinates whom they viewed as less than fully adult. Indians did not even have control over the so-called Indian Republics, which were endowed with communal land and a town center and church, but where everything down to the grid pattern of the streets was decided by the colonists. Indian nobles were given responsibility for their towns, but outside of them they had little status. In legal matters, the testimony of one Spanish man outweighed the countertestimony of four Indian men, although Indians did have the right to appeal cases to the Crown. Spanish priests at first embraced the challenge of learning native languages so that they could bring a full understanding of church doctrine to the Indians. But they eventually concluded that Indians could not be held fully responsible for backsliding into idolatry, and so exempted them from the Inquisition and limited the sacraments available to them.[9]

Indians who worked the ranches in the outermost reaches of Chiapas's colonial society were generally divorced from the collective identities, protections and responsibilities of the Indian republics. Colonial ranchers dominated the more remote town centers and held virtually unregulated feudal authority over ranch settlements. On the ranches, Indians generally subsisted as indentured laborers on plots given over to them in return for three or more days per week of labor for the ranch. Ranches were in many ways self-sufficient domains, producing cattle, sugar, and grains for trade, and provisioned occasionally by peddlers from San Cristóbal's Cuxtitali barrio. Owners generally sustained town and ranch homes, circulating between rural and town life by season. Natives on a ranch were beholden to the owner as their patrón, who in turn held substantial power over the fates of Indians of his estate. Rosario Castellanos's novel *Balún Canán* (*The Nine Guardians*) evokes a vivid sense of the oppressive life on these remote ranches, based on her childhood experience on a family ranch in the hinterlands of Comitán, where the vestiges of some ranches survive and disputes rage between landowners and the peasants who wish to take over the ranches.[10]

It was at Cancuc, a Tzeltal Indian republic on the fringes of the highlands, that Chiapas's natives mounted the region's first major Indian rebellion in 1712. The rebels rose to protest abuses by colonial Spanish authorities and ladino overlords, including priests who imposed heavy fees for administering sacraments. The uprising began as a cult based on the apparition of the Virgin to natives near Cancuc and quickly spread to nearby Tzeltal and Tzotzil communities.[11] The clergy intervened, claiming that natives were worshipping an idol. Defending their cult, the natives revolted at Cancuc, overpowering local ladinos and forcing them to take indigenous sacraments administered by self-proclaimed native clergy, one of whom declared that

> there was no longer King, tributes, *alcalde mayor* [province governor], nor officials of Ciudad Real because [the native priests] had come to free them from all this; and that there was no longer Bishop nor priest . . . ; and that [Indians] should now enjoy their ancient liberty; and . . . have only vicars and parish priests of their own who would administer all the sacraments.[12]

Explicitly renouncing the Spanish clergy and inverting the power of ladinos over Indians, the movement, in effect, declared war against the colonial regime. Colonial authorities in Ciudad Real called in troops from Guatemala to crush the rebellion, which had inspired widespread fear of a race war. Cancuc was demoted in status and did not regain its rights as a community until 1989, when President Salinas de Gortari restored it to municipal rank with much fanfare about the reestablishment of native rights.

Export Enclaves and National Consolidation

Chiapas seceded from Guatemala after Independence and joined Mexico in 1824, but it took nearly a century for the republic to integrate Chiapas and other distant states in economic and political projects of national scope.[13] The Mexican Republic abolished Indians' categorically inferior status, but their *de facto* subordination continued. In the meantime, European and North American entrepreneurs began to cash in on trade that the Spanish Crown had formerly monopolized, reorienting it to supply raw materials for new industry and foods for growing cities. In Chiapas, entrepreneurs found two valuable commodities, timber and coffee.

Figure 1.2 **Export and Development in Nineteenth Century Chiapas.**

The export of timber and coffee transformed the economic landscape of Chiapas. Indians became virtual debt slaves, working in coffee plantations along Chiapas's western coast and logging the jungles of eastern Chiapas. The central highlands surrounding San Cristóbal de las Casas lost prominence as outsiders began to exploit the lowlands to the east and west. From the nineteenth century onwards, Chiapas was characterized by this new orientation, which created divisions that persist to the present day.[14]

Imagine an invisible line running diagonally through Chiapas from the northwestern corner of the state to the southeastern corner of the state. On the left of this line is the relatively prosperous

Soconusco coast, the fertile slopes of the Sierra Madre and the Grijalva River valley, where commercial agriculture established a strong foothold in the nineteenth century. To the east of this line lie the central highlands and the eastern lowlands, peopled largely by Indians. Far in this eastern portion of the state lie the rain forests of the *Selva Lacandona* (Lacandón jungle), which began to be stripped of old-growth mahogany trees in the 1800s and is now a barely habitable jungle, the heartland of the Zapatista movement. The two sides of Chiapas that this imaginary line represents developed in vastly different ways and have widely divergent political and cultural histories.

The logging business that developed in eastern Chiapas during the nineteenth century was controlled by Europeans and contributed little to Chiapas as a region or to Mexico as a nation. By the 1890s, European-owned logging firms were exploiting the entire drainage of the Usumacinta River and its tributaries for what historian Jan de Vos[15] has characterized as its "green gold," the prized tropical hardwoods of ancient-growth mahogany and cedar. Because both species were widely dispersed throughout the forest with perhaps one or two mature specimens per hectare, the logging firms laid claim to vast tracts along the rivers flowing through the tropical forest. They set up temporary camps along the river banks and employed chicle tappers, who gathered tree sap as a base for chewing gum, to scout for preferred timber. After felling an ancient tree, work teams with oxen would haul the trunk to a stream bed where cresting flood season waters could carry it downstream. The logging firms then trimmed and shaped giant slabs of wood for shipment to Liverpool or London to auction to furniture manufacturers throughout Europe. Once the coveted trees were harvested from a tract of land, firms relocated their campsites. Indian workers, who were held in virtual servitude through debts to the company stores providing them with food and drink, moved with them. This type of industry, which extracted the desired trees and then moved on, left behind no settlements and no roads, railways or other productive infrastructure in the eastern lowlands.

The development of coffee plantations in Chiapas's western mountains did contribute to the growth of Chiapas's regional economy. The plantations arose after the California gold rush in mid-nineteenth century when ships transporting miners around Cape Horn and up the Pacific coast to California provided a way to ship raw materials and foodstuffs to the northern Atlantic ports. Foreign entrepreneurs (primarily Germans) profited from this sudden accessibility to Atlantic markets by investing in coffee plantations. The steep, fertile slopes of the Sierra Madre along Chiapas's Soconusco coast were ideal for coffee growing and huge plantations were established.[16]

As a result, the lowland Grijalva River valley, which supplied the coffee plantations with food and draft animals, emerged as a dynamic center of commercial agriculture in the last half of the nineteenth century, and the ranchers who established farms there began to compete with and displace the older oligarchy of the central highlands. This competition sharpened as the two groups took opposite sides in a debate raging between the Mexican Conservatives, who wanted to preserve the prerogatives of the Church and the military, and the Mexican Liberals, who wanted to free up Church lands for entrepreneurial development. As the debate escalated into civil war, the elites of the central highlands, anxious to preserve their control over the highland economy and its native labor, sided with the Conservatives. The lowland ranchers, who coveted the Church-held estates in the Grijalva valley, sided with the Liberals. The Liberals won and in 1863 the Church was divested of its land, which was put up for sale. The Liberals of Chiapas moved the seat of state government west to lowland Chiapa de Corzo in 1869 and to Tuxtla Gutiérrez not long after, further undercutting the power of their highland rivals.

The indigenous people of Chiapas were often the pawns and victims of the Liberal-Conservative rivalry, especially during the French Intervention of 1861 to 1867, when both sides drafted Indians as porters and soldiers and taxed them. The Liberals tried to set natives against the highland Conservatives and the Church by apprising natives of their right to worship freely and their lack of obligation to pay church taxes. Once again, as in 1712, a cult arose among the indigenous people of the highlands, this time centered in the Tzotzil community of Chamula. Alarmed in light of the 1712 rebellion, the elite of San Cristóbal attacked the cult's shrine in 1868 and jailed its leader. This did not deter devotees, however, as the cult spread to neighboring communities. A Liberal schoolteacher warned the Chamulas of an impending confrontation and persuaded them to march peacefully to San Cristóbal in 1869 to negotiate with authorities there. Unfortunately, it was too late. Ladino hysteria had risen to a fever pitch and several hundred Indians marched into a massacre.[17]

Meanwhile, the Liberals enacted a series of laws that made it possible for non-Indians to purchase communal lands held by impoverished native communities. In the highlands, profiteers quickly bought up such land and established private ranches in the former Indian republics, which forced many Indians to either work at the bidding of ranchers who took over their lands or to seek their livelihoods elsewhere. Consequently, large segments of the indigenous population worked on the coffee plantations of the Soconusco or the ranches of the Grijalva River valley, where they invariably labored for a pittance and were trapped into a cycle of working to pay off debts.[18]

Taxes imposed by the state government late in the century were another mechanism through which ranchers induced Indians to enter poorly remunerated labor on the plantations. Head taxes, police levies, school contributions, and other local government charges amounted to about forty days' wages for a rural worker. Indians who could not pay were charged additional fines, leaving them with no alternative but to sell their labor to *enganchadores*—professional agents who advanced debtors loans and sent them to work off their debts on plantations or on urban construction projects. The Grijalva valley plantations obtained many laborers from such tools of Liberalism, as did the coffee planters of the Soconusco, who would contract native laborers through highland ranch owners.[19]

Liberal use of the law to promote business and commercial agriculture accelerated under dictator Porfirio Díaz, who held the presidency for six terms from 1876 to 1910. Díaz allowed foreign and national entrepreneurs to take advantage of laws designed to free up land, labor, and natural resources. Díaz's policies, which were similar in spirit to the open-market restructuring now being promoted by the Salinas de Gortari government, did spur development, but often at the expense of villages and communities throughout Mexico whose lands the developers absorbed and whose citizens became impoverished workers.

Chiapas was drawn into Porfirian development during the 1890s, after Guatemala constructed a railway from its western coast to the Atlantic Ocean in order to reduce the cost of transporting its coffee harvest by sea. Concerned that the Soconusco plantation owners would try to secede from Mexico and rejoin Guatemala in order to take advantage of the railway, the Mexican government acted forcefully to integrate the region into the national economy by building a railway along the Pacific coast for the ranchers in northwestern and central Chiapas to ship their goods into the heart of the country. As a result, western and central Chiapas became firmly connected to the rest of Mexico.[20] Eastern Chiapas, however, remained a remote and undeveloped part of the state, a condition that persisted until the Zapatista rebels called attention to the plight of the region in 1994.

Mexico's Revolution

When Mexicans speak of their Revolution, they refer not only to the civil war that lasted from 1910 to 1917, but also to the government's implementation, over a period of many decades, of the political and social reforms contained in the 1917 Constitution.[21]

All told, the 1917 Constitution was perhaps the most progressive constitution of its era in its call for fair elections, adequate wages and proper conditions for workers, land for peasants, and other reforms. But Mexico's constitution, like all Latin American constitutions written within the framework of the civil law system, sets forth *ideals* toward which the government should strive, rather than iron-clad *guarantees* promised by common law Anglo Saxon constitutions.[22] What the Mexican constitution promises and what the national and state governments legislate and actually (if ever) deliver are two different things. The present-day Zapatistas, who are calling for a new constitutional convention, claim the 1917 Constitution's promises are not being met and never will be.[23]

The Revolution came to Chiapas in 1914, when followers of the revolutionary hero Venustiano Carranza arrived and imposed a state law abolishing debt servitude. Thousands of indentured native workers were freed from the ranches where they toiled and allowed to return to their homes in the highlands.[24] This radical move changed the status quo for some indigenous workers and poor mestizos, although it did not affect workers on the more remote ranches and plantations in eastern Chiapas.

Freeing the workers, however, angered Chiapas's landholding factions in both the western part of the state and the highlands and inspired them to bury differences and unite to "defend" Chiapas against the revolutionaries. The landowners recruited armed gangs to carry out guerilla missions against the revolutionaries. Nicknamed the *Mapaches* (raccoons) for their nighttime military forays and their habit of foraging in peasant cornfields, these gangs waged war against the revolutionary regime for six years, eventually defeating them with the help of impoverished peasants who were pressed into joining the cause. The new government was forced to accommodate the Mapaches and even appointed one of them to be governor of Chiapas, thus leaving power in the hands of landowners.[25]

As a result, the reforms of the Revolution came slowly to Chiapas. Some scholars have argued that, in effect, the Revolution never reached Chiapas at all.[26] While this overstates the case, it is true that reforms were unevenly implemented.

By the late 1920s, some peasants, emboldened by the changes sweeping the country, began to press local elites to comply with new government policies that granted indigenous people and rural workers basic rights. Workers in the Soconusco coffee plantations, for example, participated in Socialist-led labor organizing.[27] In the decade that followed, some of the elites who had sponsored the Mapaches were gradually forced to acknowledge the primacy of the national government as it implemented labor and agrarian reform and established policies that protected Indians.

The situation was quite different on the isolated plantations and ranches of the south and east, where Indians continued to labor in debt peonage for more than a decade after the practice was outlawed and where reformers faced entrenched and recalcitrant ranchers. Such landowners, who had long been allowed to rule the state with a brutal hand, were secure in both their command over the region's poor and their isolation from the capital. They were not inclined to publicize the new laws coming out of Mexico City and knew, too, that no one was likely to interfere when they delayed the implementation of reforms required by the central government.

Students of American history may find a parallel in the experience of some black communities immediately after the Civil War, when African Americans in remote parts of the South remained in slavery, ignorant of the fact that the Emancipation Proclamation had been signed, ostensibly freeing them from their bondage. Former Confederates withheld the news and so black Americans had to begin a second campaign—one of information—before they were able to claim the liberation that was supposed to be theirs already. The situation was similar in eastern Chiapas, where peasants had to first educate themselves about the changes in law and then demand that landowners honor them. The politicians proclaimed justice for the poor, but it took many years for the day-to-day experience of most peasants to change for the better. Not until the 1930s did peasants in the furthest reaches of the state inform themselves about their rights and organize themselves into groups to demand compliance from the landlords.

When the newly-politicized peasants began to clash with the entrenched elites of eastern Chiapas, who had taken their power for granted for so long, the social order of the countryside changed drastically. In *Balún Canán (The Nine Guardians)*, Rosario Castellanos wrote poignantly about these clashes as they were played out on a vast plantation near the border of southeastern Chiapas. She recounts the story of a Ladino rancher who responds to government pressure to provide a school for the Tzeltal Indian children on his estate by hiring a barely literate paperboy to be the teacher. The young man, totally unsuited for this task and unable to communicate in Tzeltal, begins drinking heavily and beating the children. The Indians come to demand a new teacher, but are rebuffed by the landlord. Eventually, the teacher is killed, the plantation owner leaves for his city home, and the school is abandoned.

Although fictional, this tale portrays the type of interaction that characterized relationships in the outback of Chiapas during the decades following the Revolution. The government did little to ensure that its ostensibly pro-peasant reforms, such as mandatory schooling, were carried out properly. What compliance there was tended to be the result of Indian agitation, not governmental enforcement. And while indigenous people often ended up realizing little in the way of concrete gains from their confrontations with powerful landowners, they did manage to put the ladinos on the defensive, and thus began, in a gradual way, to transform the nature of power on the plantations. The conflict between rancher and peasant in eastern Chiapas is not simply a story of the past, however, as it is one of the ongoing concerns that the EZLN says galvanized them to rebel.

In western Chiapas, in contrast to the center and east, relations between peasants and landowners gradually improved after the Revolution. Without a ready supply of laborers, plantation owners began to rent plots of land to their former workers in order to bring in the harvest. This new arrangement, similar to sharecropping, was still exploitative, but preferable to the more coercive previous system. Peasants were able to live in their own homes with their own families and were able to farm their plots of land as they saw fit. Being able to rent small parcels of land may not seem like much of an opportunity, but peasants were enormously creative in turning their farming into small-scale entrepreneurial ventures.

In addition, social interactions between landowners and workers underwent a metamorphosis as the master-servant relationship evolved into more of a patron-client relationship. Although the relationship was unequal, it allowed for more social interaction; it was not uncommon, for example, for peasants to ask landlords to be godparents to their children. This social background is important because it helps explain why peasant-landowner relationships are still less conflictual in western Chiapas than in the east. Contemporary landlords in the Soconusco area and Grijalva River valley continue to portray themselves as more progressive than landlords in other parts of the state.

Agrarian Reform

During the 1930s, under the administration of President Lázaro Cárdenas, the government redistributed thousands of hectares of land in Chiapas. This was by no means a wholesale reorganization, since many large estates remained intact, but it did provide dozens of indigenous communities with their own land.

It is difficult to overstate the power of land reform in winning peasants to the side of the State. Even when land grants were agonizingly slow in coming—and they often were—the federal government was able to hold out the *promise* of land reform as a

way of retaining peasant loyalty. By positioning itself, at least symbolically, as the champion of peasants and the poor, the government was able to inspire tremendous popular support for its
programs. Understanding the importance of land reform is thus
critical in explaining why Chiapas has remained a relatively calm
area, except for a few outbursts of political violence, during most
of this century.[28]

How was peace maintained in this region that seemed to have
so many factors—poverty, discrimination, injustice—pulling it
toward revolution? The answer lies partially in the isolation of
Indian hamlets and partially in the national government's shrewd
use of various redistributive policies that brought one peasant
group after another into the system. While the government did not
eliminate the discrimination and injustice that plagued Indians
and poor peasants, it did offer them the chance, at least in theory,
to farm their own land.

By coopting one group after another with land redistribution,
the government ensured that the peasants' primary loyalty would
be to the state and not to their class. The factionalism that developed as each community struggled for its own land helped to con-
tain the potential for organized dissidence because it meant that
each village or *municipio* (township) concentrated more on maintaining strong ties with the national government than with other
native communities that might well compete for the same land.

It is important to note that the government's emphasis on land
reform was not just a bid to win the support of the peasantry. It was
also the basis of a strategy for development rooted in agrarian economics that took shape after the American stock market collapsed
in 1929. The worldwide depression that ensued sharply curtailed
the demand for Mexican exports, resulting in the loss of foreign
capital the government depended upon to fund industrial development. To compensate for this loss, the Cárdenas administration
instituted a six-year plan to replace the export-oriented economy
with new domestic industrialization predicated on peasant production of cheap food. The government began to expropriate land
from stagnant commercial estates to turn over to *ejidos* (lands
vested in peasant communities by agrarian reform). On the ejidos,
peasant families could join to farm collectively if necessary—
arrangements that required minimal capital investment. The huge

scale of peasant production kept down the price of foodstuffs, which allowed urban-sector wages to be kept low enough for new industry start-up. At the same time, peasants' income from crop sales financed their consumption of manufactured goods, securing a domestic market for the new industries. This approach prefigured the import substitution industrialization strategy of most Latin American countries in subsequent decades and brought Mexico several decades of growth.[29]

Figure 1.3 **Agrarian Reform in Chiapas.** Most land redistributed by 1950 dates from the 1934–40 presidency of Lázaro Cárdenas. By 1975, agrarian reform had spread into eastern Chiapas. Large private landholdings remain primarily in western Chiapas where cattle ranching and commercial farming prevail.

Photo 1.1 **Agrarian Colonists.** Men meet under a tree in one of Chiapas's numerous agrarian colonies to discuss *ejidal* business.

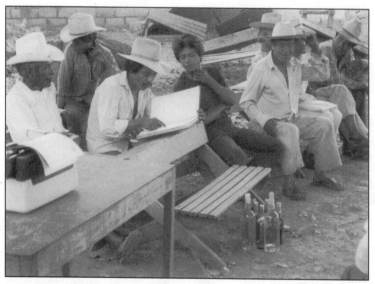

Photo 1.2 *Ejidal* **Assembly.** Those in assembly consume liquor at the end of the meeting to affirm agreements.

As the government began to expropriate land, it also encouraged peasant groups to stake their own claims by occupying and retaking land occupied by private estates and plantations. This tactic not only relieved the government of the burden of having to go on the offensive with landowners, but also ensured that peasants would be more personally invested in the creation of a new economic order. As peasants agitated for land reform, they were brought in to new political organizations, such as the populist Partido Revolucionaro Mexicano (which was later renamed the Institutional Revolutionary Party or PRI) that had been set up to help orchestrate the peasants' demands, ensuring that they matched the goals of the state.

In Chiapas, Cárdenas's policies firmly established the government as an ally of Indians and peasants against the landowners in the central highlands. Cárdenas rallied indigenous and peasant voters around his candidate for the Chiapas gubernatorial elections in 1936, recruiting voters through a former labor commissioner, Erasto Urbina, who spoke Tzeltal and Tzotzil and had good contacts with Indians throughout the region. Cárdenas then rewarded the indigenous and peasant voters by establishing Urbina as director of a new Department of Indian Protection. Urbina helped his supporters initiate and win claims under agrarian reform, redistributing a substantial amount of land in the highlands and in the Soconusco. Urbina also set up an Indian-run indigenous workers' union with monopoly power to recruit labor from the highlands for coastal coffee plantations. These measures established powerful and long-lasting indigenous and peasant loyalties for the ruling party.[30]

As the 1930s drew to a close and World War II broke out, Mexico once again found itself scrambling to meet U.S. demand for fruits, vegetables, fibers, and textiles. This macroeconomic shift had important consequences for Indians, peasants, and small farmers because the government once again enacted policies that favored the development of large-scale commercial agriculture to meet the sudden demand for exports. The new flow of foreign capital helped the state finance infrastructure, such as irrigation systems, that made large-scale farming viable, especially in the northern part of the country. These changes brought land reform to an abrupt halt and disappointed peasants' expectations of further land redistribution. In some cases, gains made under Lázaro Cárdenas were actually reversed and the types of estates that he had once dismantled prospered again.

Meanwhile, the government continued to develop domestic industry by holding down the relative price of food. As mentioned previously, inexpensive food translated into a subsidy for industrial employers who could thus pay lower wages, but it was a subsidy provided by peasants. Under Cárdenas, many peasants had given up traditional crafts and used manufactured wares when given land to farm. As fiscal policy allowed manufactured items to rise in price more rapidly than food, peasants had to intensify their production simply to make ends meet.[31]

To meet the rising cost of living, many peasants cultivated their land to the limits of its capacity and augmented their income by working part-time in the reviving sector of commercial agriculture. Because their own cultivation assured subsistence, many peasants worked for less-than-subsistence wages, which in turn held down wages throughout the economy. As the 1940s drew to a close, many peasants found they were no longer able to focus exclusively on the production of crops. Their numbers swelled, and some peasants began to seek land in eastern Chiapas.

The state's attention to Chiapas's Indians waned during the 1940s, then waxed during the 1950s as the government promoted Indian development projects to curry favor that had been secured with earlier agrarian reform. Endeavors aimed at Indians dated back to the Cárdenas presidency. In 1940, Mexico hosted the first Interamerican Indian Congress and Indians from all over Mexico were invited to attend. As a result of the Congress, Mexico and other Latin American countries established national Indian institutes. Mexico's National Indianist Institute (INI), became the channel through which major funding for rural development was administered, heightening the status of Indians as special clients of the state.

INI officials acknowledged that their goals—rural development through education, improved health, and extension agriculture—were the same as for peasants generally, but that the special characteristics of Indians in regions such as central Chiapas required distinctive efforts to integrate Indian communities into the national agrarian sector. INI sought out Indian leaders to train as *promotores* (local agents) of community development and used them to organize work crews for road construction, to teach curricula designed specially for Indian school children, to run small clinics and promote public sanitation, and to demonstrate new crops and cultivation techniques. In effect, Indian promotores became brokers with a good deal of discretion over who would receive development resources, and through them the state sustained its control over local-level politics.[32]

By making the municipio the entity through which development programs were channeled, the government helped to unify those within communities while heightening separation between them. As a consequence, Indian communities remained quite isolated and parochial. Indianist programs, furthermore, reinforced the identity of indigenous people as Indians rather than as part of the class of poor rural workers and peasants. Such identity is part of what has led traditionalists in highland communities like Zinacantán and Chamula, which are closely allied with the PRI, to eschew the Zapatistas. In eastern Chiapas, by contrast, the Zapatistas draw upon the perception of shared interests held by peasants and Indians.

As we shall see in chapters to come, agrarian reform and Indianism were not the only ways in which the national government secured support from the exploited rural poor. During the oil boom of the 1970s, Mexico bought popular support by funneling money into development projects and public works. But land reform remained prominent in the public agenda—and in the popular consciousness—as the most cherished legacy of the Mexican Revolution.

When President Salinas de Gortari suspended land reform in 1992, he not only deprived many peasants of their hopes of ever farming their own land, he also may have compromised the peace that has held sway in the countryside for most of this century.

II. EASTERN CHIAPAS: LAND

Few frontiers remain for those in search of land. The Selva Lacandona is one of them. Since the 1950s, it has served as a last refuge for impoverished peasants seeking land. The rank and file of Zapatistas are peasants who have embraced the opportunities and the travails of colonizing one of the world's last remaining rain forests. They have endured the same adversity that tropical frontiers pose for settlers from other areas—poor soils, unfamiliar and poisonous plants and animals, skin-burrowing insects and parasitic diseases—and suffer opposition from ranchers who control the best land in the region. In recent years, peasants have found it harder and harder to establish homesteads because significant areas of the forest have been set aside as nature reserves. A scramble for land has led to conflicts between peasant and rancher, and between peasant and peasant. Conflict in the region has been exacerbated first by the government's arbitrary recognition of certain peasant settlements over others and then by agrarian laws that prevented peasants from making further land claims.

It is not surprising that activists, whether Protestant missionaries, Catholic liberation theologians, or political unionizers, have found a ready audience in eastern Chiapas, where the government has encouraged people to settle, even though there are few roadways, no urban centers, and pitifully few public services.

Colonizing Eastern Chiapas

In the past four decades, peasant colonization has brought dramatic change to the Selva Lacandona. The two maps in Figure 2.1 underscore this change.

The first map is drawn from information agrarian reform officials compiled in 1953 and reveals a largely untapped, rugged tropical forest, sparsely populated by Lacandón Indians.[1] Logging spread from the Usumacinta River up its tributaries beginning in

38

Figure 2.1 **Eastern Chiapas Land Tenure, 1953 and 1991.** Ranches and logging concessions on national lands dominated the eastern Chiapas landscape in 1950. At that time, peasants held *ejidal* grants only in the Ocosingo valley. By 1991, the government had granted peasants title to agrarian colonies throughout eastern Chiapas (illustrated only for the easternmost region), even within the Montes Azul bioreserve.

the late nineteenth century until 1949, when the Mexican government declared timber to be a national resource and suspended the logging rights of private corporations. Ranches spread from the outer concentric ring of the old colonial zone into the Ocosingo region and down some of the higher valleys toward the Usumacinta. The only peasant holdings in 1953 were *ejidos* that the government had set up under 1930s agrarian reform in the higher western valleys close to the township centers of Ocosingo and Altamirano.

Forty years later, the picture has changed drastically. The second map, created in 1991, unveils a mosaic of peasant colonies pressing into the rain forest from the north, west, and south. The Montes Azul and Lacan Tun bioreserves that the government established in the *municipio* of Ocosingo are most of what remains of the Selva Lacandona.

Peasants in eastern Chiapas hold proportionately more land under agrarian code provisions than almost any other region of the state. But the land they hold is often barely arable, heightening tensions between peasants, agrarian reform authorities, and ranchers in the region. Much land in Chiapas is still held privately in large ranches, but such ranches are found mostly in other regions—in the Grijalva River valley, in Cintalapa, and in neighboring townships in the western part of the state (see Figure 1.3 in previous chapter).

Another irony, and one of the major sources of conflict in eastern Chiapas, is that although peasants now dominate its landscape, they do not control local government; instead it continues to be dominated by ranchers and large landowners. In this respect, eastern Chiapas differs markedly from central highland Chiapas, where Indians who benefited from agrarian reform also control their own town governments.[2]

This disjunction of power can be traced back to the unfolding of peasant colonization in the northern and western parts of eastern Chiapas, which began in the 1930s when resident workers on ranches began to seek lands on the peripheries of large estates, particularly in Las Margaritas, Ocosingo, and Altamirano. Although the government did establish some ejidos near Ocosingo and Altamirano, many ranchers accommodated "their" workers by selling them marginal lands on the fringes of their properties, thus forestalling expropriation and creating buffers of friendly peasant communities that they could control through patronage.

This tactic also helped ensure a ready supply of labor for the ranchers, who needed workers to herd livestock overland for export through Tabasco; to plant, harvest, and refine sugar; and to cultivate and transport citrus and other crops. Peasants were offered the use of small tracts to farm in exchange for three days work on the ranch. Such alliances between private landowners and peasants both blurred and complicated lines of potential conflict, eventually igniting feuds not only between ranchers and workers, but also between groups of peasants allied with different landlords. Conflicts sharpened with the passage of time as colonists outstripped their resources and began to press for more land for their maturing families.

Unión Juárez, a peasant settlement located on the fringes of the Sibacá valley in northern Ocosingo, exemplifies the type of conflict prevalent in regions dominated by ranchers. Unión Juárez was settled by a small group of families from the town of Tenango and the ranches of Metzá and La Gloria who banded together to purchase two adjacent tracts from separate ranch owners in 1972. By selling the tracts to these aspiring smallholders, the ranch owners forestalled takeover of the tracts by ejidal colonists from Sibacá who had petitioned the agrarian reform authorities for enlargement of their holdings. Initially, nine families shared the Unión Juárez holding. By 1987, however, when liberation theologian Brother Pablo Iribarren Pascal visited Unión Juárez on a pastoral mission, the smallholders had come into conflict with neighboring ranchers and colonists by appealing to the agrarian reform authorities for lands for their children, who had matured, and whose young families Unión Juárez could no longer accommodate. One of the parishioners told Iribarren about the opposition claimants encountered from ranchers and other peasants.

> We asked for lands, and an engineer came out to identify national lands we could claim, two parcels, one of 50 hectares and the other 20 hectares. But when he came out to survey the parcels, we were set upon by people from the surrounding colonies and ranches, who had been roused by the owner of the Pomalá ranch to thwart our claim. They attacked us with clubs, rifles, and machetes and took the engineer and one of our families prisoner to the settlement at Gethsemaní. People from Batel, Gethsemaní, and Ocotal, all of them Protestant towns, were among those who ganged up on us. In

Gethsemaní, they chopped up our clothes, shoes, and hats with machetes. We were sent to Ocosingo, where we were kept in prison for three days while a representative of the Socialist Workers Party (PST) whom we got word to, worked to get us out. The jailing cowed us, we're afraid to pursue the claim with the *Reforma Agraria* and are thinking about getting credits so that we can buy the land and get it without having further problems with neighboring colonists and ranchers.[3]

Colonization came to the region's eastern and southern frontiers when migrants from other parts of the state and from other provinces of Mexico began to arrive and establish settlements in the 1950s. For the most part, these settlers leapfrogged over the ranches of the north and west and began to colonize the tropical forest. Although peasants predominate in these remote areas far from any township seat, they gain little benefit from the infrastructure and services that the government channels through town governments.

Many of the newcomers were Tzeltal and Tzotzil Indians from the central highlands of Chiapas; others were Tojolobales and Choles whose ancestors had worked for ranchers in the outer tier of Chiapas's colonial economy. Since colonial times when conquistadors regrouped decimated native populations in the Chiapas highlands, the highlands have served as a reserve of Indian labor. When Indians began to recover demographically in the nineteenth century, they held so little land for subsistence in the highlands that they had to work on lowland ranches and plantations. Chiapas's populations have grown substantially since 1900, creating further hardships for the already land-poor Indians.[4] Agrarian reform helped abate this pressure temporarily in the 1930s and 1940s, but by the 1950s highland Indians were once again outgrowing their land and Indian men began to work in the developed agrarian economies of the central Grijalva Valley and the Soconusco. After 1950, indigenous people from many highland communities uprooted their families and ventured into the forests of eastern Chiapas in search of land to colonize and farm.[5]

Figure 2.2 **Colonization and Landscape Changes in Eastern Chiapas.** As migrants from the highlands of Chiapas, as well as from other states, set up colonies in eastern Chiapas, grasslands displaced tropical forests.

Newcomers from other states joined the highland Indians to colonize the Selva Lacandona in the 1970s, responding to then-president Luis Echeverría's efforts to appease peasant dissidents in other parts of the country with agrarian reform and colonization. Echeverría became president two years after the 1968 massacre of student activists in Mexico's Tlatelolco Square prior to the Olympics, which students had threatened to disrupt. Many held Echeverría, Minister of Interior in 1968, responsible for the bloodshed. To help polish his image when he became president, Echeverría embraced populist programs and sought the support of peasants, many of whom had been organized by remnants of the student movement in central and northern Mexico. He pressed forward with agrarian reform and opened uncolonized land in Mexico's south to peasants from other areas. Under Echeverría's policies, newcomers came to eastern Chiapas from nearby Tabasco and Campeche, but also from Quintana Roo, Yucatán, Veracruz, Puebla, and Guerrero, Morelos, and Oaxaca, from the federal district, Hidalgo, Jalisco, and Michoacán in central and western Mexico, and even from Sinaloa and Sonora in the northwest.[6]

By 1980, settlers from other states accounted for just over 7 percent of the population of Ocosingo, the highest proportion of any rural municipality in Chiapas. In the early 1980s, officials invited additional out-of-state colonists in to help fill the vacuum of settlement near the border with Guatemala and thus prevent the incursion of Guatemalan refugees, whom the government confined to border camps.

The settlers converged on the tropical forest from the north and west along roadways and trails blazed by government-sanctioned logging, settling on unclaimed national lands or on tracts with prior claims. During the 1950s, for example, peasants from ranches in the Patihuitz Canyon region took over lands that had once belonged to the Bulnes logging firms, claiming them as national lands. Finally, in the 1960s, they received title for them under agrarian reform as expropriations from oversize timbering estates.[7] Timbering firms had allowed many such tracts to fall into arrears in taxes. When families from several different areas banded together to establish the settlement of Ch'um Cerro on other Bulnes lands in the 1960s, they learned from agrarian officials that the Bulnes firm had neglected for twenty-five years to pay taxes for the land on which the colonists happened to settle, and that the settlers could take over in 1970 under a provisional agrarian grant.

Like most tropical rain forests, the Selva Lacandona of eastern Chiapas is a paradise only for those who know how to respect its limitations. Its biomass consists of highly diverse species spread through multiple canopies that protect relatively thin soils from the rapid degradation to which they are prone when exposed to tropical sun. Long-term tropical forest dwellers, such as eastern Chiapas's Lacandón Indians, cultivate by thinning, but not destroying the multi-tiered canopy and by introducing or nurturing useful species in small and multi-cropped clearings. Skilled cultivators, such as José Camino Viejo, a Lacandón Indian from

Mensabak described by anthropologist-conservationist James D. Nations, raise as many as seventy-nine different crops of food and fiber, more for family use than for sale. In his multi-canopied farm plot of 3 hectares, Camino produced corn, beans, and squash, but also rice, pineapples, sugarcane, bananas, taro, manioc, yams, limes, spices, oranges, cotton, avocados, rubber, cacao, and tobacco.[8]

Newcomers to the region, by contrast, usually introduced intensive cultivation of *milpa* (the traditional peasant cornfield) appropriate to the higher, cooler climate and richer soils of their original homelands. Having worked in zones of commercial agriculture, they also brought familiarity with cattle and cash crops such as coffee. Producing first for subsistence and then for commercial markets, settlers soon exhausted the land and were forced to press deeper and deeper into the forest. Satellite images of eastern Chiapas starkly reveal this relentless and irreversible march, which has turned wide swaths of the rain forest into grassland suitable only for grazing cattle.

The example of Nuevo Huistán, peopled by Tzotzil speakers from the highland township of Huistán, illustrates how colonists introduced grasslands as they effected the shift from subsistence to commercial farming. Huistecos migrated on foot, with the few possessions they could carry by tumpline, and established Nuevo Huistán in the 1960s on the steep slopes of one of the Las Margaritas canyons.[9] The first to arrive established themselves by working for settlers in nearby, older colonies in exchange for food and a supply of seed that allowed them to begin farming on their own. Once established in subsistence farming, the founding families served as hosts for later-arriving Huistecos; the settlement grew to sixty-three households and won rights to 1940 hectares authorized by agrarian authorities. Meanwhile, the founders planted coffee for commercial sale as well as cacao, citrus, and other crops. They also seeded a third of their cultivated land in pasture for cattle and other livestock. By 1983, the colony derived seven-eighths of its income from cash crops and cattle, horses, and mules.[10] A 1990 survey of the surrounding zone showed that pasture, much of it induced, made up 60 percent of nonidle acreage, coffee about 10 percent, and subsistence cropping of corn and beans not more than 30 percent.[11]

Over time, Nuevo Huistán emerged as a node linking commerce from the Las Margaritas canyon region outward to a roadway built by the government to control the Guatemalan border. It
is important to note that the settlement's increasingly commercial
orientation separated settlers (who for the most part had begun
production on roughly equal allotments of land) into two groups,
one of poorer settlers who relied on subsistence farming and wage
work for other compatriots, and a wealthier group involved in marketing cash crops and cattle. When one considers that wealthier
colonists attained economies of scale from collective herding and
commercial marketing,[12] the distinction between them and private
ranchers begins to blur. Such differentiation, which we will discuss
further in Chapter Four, creates incentives for relative "have-nots"
to undertake new colonization of their own, and feeds tensions
inherent in the multiple and often conflicting claims of colonists
seeking legal authorization for new and supplemental land.

Agrarian Reform and Conflict

In 1992, the Mexican government rewrote the agrarian reform
section of the Mexican Constitution, bringing an end to the land
reform policies that have shaped the government's relationship to
the peasantry for half a century.[13] In Chiapas, where many land
claims have yet to be resolved after languishing in the state bureaucracy for years, the repeal of land reform legislation robbed many
peasants not just of the possibility of gaining a piece of land, but,
quite simply, of hope.[14] Sub-Comandante Marcos, in an interview
published in *Tiempo*,[15] indicated that the change in Article 27 was
the straw that broke the camel's back in persuading Zapatistas to
take up arms.

> [The government] really screwed us, now that they destroyed
> Article 27, for which Zapata and his Revolution fought.
> Salinas de Gortari arrived on the scene with his lackeys, and
> his groups, and in a flash they destroyed it. We and our fam-
> ilies have been sold down the river, or you could say that they
> stole our pants and sold them. What can we do? We did
> everything legal that we could so far as elections and organi-
> zations were concerned, and to no avail.

Rage built up in settlements such as El Carrizal, where peasants
have waited in vain over eleven years for government resolution of

their claim to lands. El Carrizal is a community made up of former resident workers from the ranch of San Rafael near Ocosingo. In 1983, these workers learned that the land they had worked for many years as hired hands was going to be sold to other peasants, leaving them without either work or a place to live. They hastily initiated a claim of their own for San Rafael, which for two years went unheeded. In 1985, they went on strike, moved their homes to a site they could defend from expected reprisals, and renewed their claim. Once again it languished, opposed both by ranchers and by other peasant smallholders who coveted the land. Meanwhile, violence broke out. In August of 1988, El Carrizal was burned to the ground by a group of armed men who are said to have acted under the direction of ranchers in cahoots with local police and the army. With support from the Emiliano Zapata Peasant Organization (OCEZ), the El Carrizal peasants marched to San Cristóbal de las Casas, where they camped in protest in the central plaza in front of the San Nicolás church, demanding that agrarian authorities grant their claim. Early in 1989, the government affirmed El Carrizal's legal status pending resolution of the land claim and oversaw rebuilding of the settlement, but violence against El Carrizal continued. By February 1994, when *New York Times* journalist Anthony DePalma interviewed El Carrizal leaders, they still awaited government resolution of their claim.[16]

The case of El Carrizal poignantly illustrates one of the most troubling aspects of land reform—the fact that the government has sometimes taken years to recognize claims on which peasants' livelihoods depend. Once a community submitted a petition for land, petitioners often had to wait several years before the government recognized their provisional right to occupy and use the land. The process was arduous. State review boards scrutinized the eligibility of the group to ensure it was actually comprised of at least twenty peasant households. They also scrutinized any documented claims to prior ties to the land in question. Then officials surveyed land within a seven kilometer radius of the community to determine its "affectability"—was it susceptible to expropriation or available for donation to the claimants, or were there competing claims? Finally state-level authorities recommended to federal superiors whether a grant should be awarded. At that point, claimants were sometimes authorized to use land on a provisional basis. But they still had to wait for a federal review of their claim. If their claim was accepted, they awaited a presidential decree and the actual granting of title before the land was legally theirs. Needless to say, the process was often held up by countervailing claims from landowners and, occasionally, other peasant groups.

According to one study,[17] land claims involved some twenty-two different government groups and public agencies and a twenty-seven-step process requiring almost two years of bureaucratic effort, *if the claim was unopposed.* In Chiapas, according to the same study, it took an average of more than seven years for the federal government to approve claims that had already been provisionally accepted by state authorities. It is understandable that being forced to "hurry up and wait" caused tremendous strain between peasants in eastern Chiapas, who have generated hundreds of claims in recent decades, and agrarian officials. Yet it is worth noting that claims from Las Margaritas and Ocosingo, the heartland of the Zapatista movement, have actually been resolved from one to two years faster, on average, than elsewhere in Chiapas.[18]

The strain between peasants and agrarian authorities has not been, of course, unique to Chiapas. Conflicts between rural communities and land reform officials have been building since the 1970s, when peasants throughout Mexico's countryside began to lay claim to more valuable lands. Peasants, landowners, and the state generally have become more militant in the past two decades in disputes over agrarian resources.

When the Mexican government initially brought agrarian reform to the national agenda during the 1930s, peasants were relatively easy to secure as allies without upsetting private agrarian interests. Most of the land that Lázaro Cárdenas's representatives turned over to peasant communities in Chiapas was marginal land that highland ranchers had appropriated from Indian communities in the nineteenth century. When agrarian communities pushed for augmentation to these holdings in the 1950s, their needs could still be met by granting them small parcels of less valuable lands on the outskirts of plantations.

By the 1960s, it became clear that these parcels were no longer adequate and peasants began to file claims for more valuable commercial farms and plantations that earlier agrarian reform had spared. Because the law authorized claims only within seven kilometers of peasant settlements of at least twenty households, peasants had to invade coveted lands and settle on them in order to initiate the process.

I know of one such land takeover from my discussions with Zinacanteco Indians who established the Colonia Santa Rosa in the late 1960s. For years, they had weighed the prospects of taking over what were thought to be untitled national lands, but in fact claimed by ranchers. But the land was too far from home for them to claim it under the law. They had to establish a settlement there to be able to stake a claim. They organized weeks in advance of a moonless night when, sixty families strong and armed with every available shotgun and machete, they invaded the land. They hastily constructed ramshackle shelters to claim as their "settlement" and set up armed lookouts to defend against rancher reprisals. Then they sent one of their members to notify government authorities of the existence of their settlement and to demand protection while pressing their claim for land as authorized by law.

As such takeovers spread in the late 1960s, landowners called on the government to put a halt to invasions and often fought off settlers with armed force, escalating confrontation in some areas of rural Mexico to the level of guerilla warfare. In the state of Guerrero, the government used troops to repress peasants. It was in part to defuse such conflict that Luis Echeverría, president from 1970 to 1976, favored the colonization of Mexico's remaining frontiers. To mollify dissident peasant leaders, the Echeverría government also offered many of them jobs in the agrarian reform bureaucracy to help administer colonization efforts.

Ironically, the very mechanisms intended to facilitate colonization often cast the government as the enemy rather than the ally of peasants, especially when they put agrarian authorities in the contradictory roles of proprietors of national lands as well as arbiters of claims to those lands. This was especially true in the case of legislation that allowed the government to establish relocation centers on national lands to resettle colonists far from their original homelands.[19] These relocation centers sometimes helped facilitate colonization, but in other instances they seemed more to serve state interests than those of peasants.

In 1969 the government initiated a dam project at Angostura

that was to flood dozens of peasant communities in the central Grijalva River valley—all of the villages had to be relocated. Relocation inflamed agrarian conflict in Venustiano Carranza, where the government tried to place a new settlement on land that had already been in dispute between ranchers and Venustiano Carranza peasants for more than twenty-five years. After a peasant leader was assassinated in 1975 and several hundred peasants invaded the disputed land in 1976, the government sent in the army to repress the peasants.[20] As a result, Venustiano Carranza became the focal point for independent organizing against the government by the Emiliano Zapata Peasant Organization (OCEZ). Peasant protests actually derailed a government plan to build a fourth dam, the Itzantún dam in the township of Huitiupán, that would have displaced peasants from their homelands into one of the government relocation centers.[21]

Compounding conflicts over land in eastern Chiapas was the fact that the government began to mark off tracts of land to establish bioreserves, ignoring the fact that the land was already occupied by impoverished peasants who had been encouraged to colonize the region. The government first laid plans in 1968 to set aside small portions of the Selva Lacandona to protect the rain forest. But ten years later, pushed by the international environmental community and by champions of the Lacandón Maya who wanted to protect the Indians from encroachment by colonists, the government set aside another third of a million hectares as the Montes Azul bioreserve.[22] To relocate 8,000 people already living in twenty-six settlements within the limits of the Montes Azul reserve, the government set up several relocation centers.[23] Then the government set up a logging firm, the Lacandón Forestry Company (COFOLASA), ostensibly to manage the bioreserve's timber on behalf of 400 Lacandón individuals in 66 families deemed to have ancestral claims on the lands of the reserve, completely disregarding claims of 8,000 non-Lacandón Indians and peasants already settled in the area. Theoretically, proceeds from timbering were to be held in trust for the Lacandón families, but critics charge that most of the profit from COFOLASA's timbering operations in Montes Azul ended up in politicians' pockets.

Guanal is one of the peasant colonies whose lands fall within the Montes Azul bioreserve. Settled in the 1960s by colonists from several areas, Guanal joined with other colonies affected by the bioreserve to prevent authorities from surveying the reserve's boundaries and to resist relocation into the new ejidos. When Brother Pablo Iribarren visited Guanal in 1988, colonists railed against the agrarian authorities and conservationists who had tried to dislodge Guanal's residents in unsuccessful efforts to relocate them into the government ejidos. Organized with help from Catholic catechists and the peasant organization *Unión de Uniones Quiptik ta Lekubtesel* (United for Our Improvement Union of Unions), Guanal and the other Montes Azul colonies filed legal briefs against dislodgement, organized protest marches in the state capital, and harassed surveyors and public authorities who tried to persuade them to relocate:

> On one occasion, when Lic. Mario Rivera came as a government delegate to [the colony of] Pichucalco insisting that we sign papers to relocate, he was so insistent that we jailed him. When his bush pilot came to pick him up that afternoon, he found Rivera in jail, so he left. When the pilot flew back the following day, we released Rivera, and he left.
>
> Another time, this same official called us to a meeting at the schoolhouse in Guanal. He got up on a table and harangued us to sign the relocation papers. A storm was brewing, and suddenly the schoolhouse lit up, struck by a bolt of lightening. Everyone was scared, and Lic. Rivera jumped down off the table in fright. After a moment, everyone broke out into applause and began to shout, "Long live Saint Lightening! Another bolt! Another bolt! Viva!" Lic. Rivera left and never returned.[24]

The Agrarian Rehabilitation Plan (PRA) was another mechanism that the government devised to facilitate colonization, but its partisan implementation served only to turn peasants against agrarian authorities. As governor of Chiapas, General Absalón Castellanos Domínguez set up the PRA in 1984 as a program for the state to buy lands from private owners to turn over to peasants in zones where peasants and ranchers were embattled over agrarian reform. Under the PRA, the state government purchased just over 80,000 hectares of private land in various parts of Chiapas to turn over to 159 peasant settlements. But the beneficiaries were overwhelmingly peasant communities affiliated with the ruling party's National Peasant Confederation (CNC). Peasant communities affiliated with independent organizations *not* aligned with the ruling party were almost completely excluded from the benefits of the PRA, even though many such peasants had prior claims on ranches bought out with PRA funding.[25]

Rather than allaying conflict, the effect of the PRA was to inflame peasants against the ruling party, agrarian authorities, and the state governor. Peasants' anger was reinforced when it became known that the governor had issued ranchers 2,932 *certificados de inafectabilidad* (exemptions protecting property from expropriation under agrarian reform) for some 1.2 million hectares of commercial farmland and ranchland in the state of Chiapas. One can begin to understand why the Zapatistas later kidnapped Absalón Castellanos and held him prisoner on charges of having betrayed the public trust.

Government intervention into the colonization of one of Mexico's last frontiers thus subtly but irrevocably reversed earlier perceptions of agrarian authorities as allies. The government replaced large landowners as the hated enemy by taking over their role. First, the state came to act as a self-interested proprietor of national lands rather than a facilitator of peasant needs. It set bioreserves off-limits to peasants, exacerbating the pressures on remaining lands. Second, the government, by rewarding peasants loyal to the ruling party, set peasants against peasants, just as hated landlords had once conceded marginal lands to "their" peasants as a bulwark against the claims of other peasants in the earlier phases of agrarian reform. And finally, in 1992, the government changed the law to put an end to the very claims it had encouraged peasants to make as colonists on the final frontier.

III. EASTERN CHIAPAS: THE BUILDING OF SOCIAL MOVEMENTS

The Zapatistas have not provided a detailed history of their origins. We know from Sub-Comandante Marcos's interviews with journalists[1] that the Zapatistas began organizing to go underground in 1983 and that certain other highly politicized peasant groups were also active at this time, but we don't know which, if any, of these groups became the Zapatista National Liberation Army. It seems most likely that the Zapatistas drew strength from various factions of peasant groups who were dissatisfied not only with the government but with other peasant organizations as well. In this chapter, we'll explore the sometimes unintentional role civil and religious movements played in orienting peasants toward political activism, and we'll examine the rise of independent peasant organizations in the eastern part of the state. We hope to illuminate the milieu in which the early Zapatista movement began, rather than offer a precise chronology of its development.

Although the Zapatistas did not burst onto the international scene until 1994, their presence in eastern Chiapas had already been an open secret for several years. Even before anyone knew the name of the Zapatista National Liberation Army, people in Ocosingo, Las Margaritas, and Altamirano spoke to journalists about the "armed groups" operating in their midst. In June of 1993, *Proceso*, a progressive Mexican weekly magazine, reported that after five years of denial, the government "acknowledged evidence that there are guerrillas in Chiapas." In August 1993, the Mexico City newspaper *La Jornada* published interviews with government officials and a Protestant pastor in eastern Chiapas who had heard gunshots in the night, witnessed arms trading, and heard stories about peasants who had been invited to join an "armed uprising" over a period of at least two years. A representative of a local peasant organization told the paper that "the existence of guerrillas is not a rumor; it has been proven that there are well-armed guerrillas operating near the Guatemalan border and it is known that they have training grounds." In September, a Jesuit priest from the Selva Lacandona told *Proceso* that he had been aware of militant armed groups assembling in the area for *eight* years.[2]

What led to the formation of this revolutionary underground in eastern Chiapas? Conservatives tend to point their fingers at the Catholic Church, which, in Chiapas, has been heavily influenced by liberation theology and has, in recent years, been at the center of social justice movements throughout the state. The Mexican government has claimed that the rebellion was instigated by "foreigners," by which they meant Guatemalan or other Central American revolutionaries. Scholars who have studied the region speculate that the Zapatistas are the outgrowth of the independent and mostly left-oriented peasant organizations that formed during the 1970s.[3] Sub-Comandante Marcos himself has hinted that the Zapatistas began ten years ago when a small group of urban intellectuals arrived in Chiapas with the specific goal of fomenting revolution.[4]

The Zapatistas have been portrayed as a group of peasants pushed to the breaking point by poverty and exploitation who finally struck out against their oppressors—the government that abandoned them, the army that repressed them, the wealthy ranchers and *caciques* (political bosses) who kept them in subjugation, the ladinos who taunted them. The Popular media have recounted stories about the hardships of life in eastern Chiapas, including the coffee that was planted and couldn't be sold, the land erosion, the brutality of ranchers, the hunger, the lack of medical care, and the inadequate education. As one reads these chronicles of misery, one can understand why the peasants finally boiled over with anger. The problem with this portrayal, however, is that it makes the rebellion appear to be a spontaneous reaction to injustice when, in fact, a group of organizers had been planning revolution for more than a decade.

Many people tend to forget that the Zapatista uprising was not the first peasant uprising in Chiapas, it was just the first to gain international attention. And while poverty and exploitation may be the rallying cries of the rebels, the movement also developed in counterpoint to the dozens of other peasant organizations operating in the state. In other words, the Zapatistas are not just fighting what they have termed the corrupt government of President Salinas, they are placing themselves in opposition to the tactics used by other peasant groups and are fighting to be the voice of the oppressed. The Zapatista consciousness was formed not just by the backbreaking toil of colonizing the Selva Lacandona, but also by dialogue and dissension within and between other peasant organizations. By taking over the town hall of San Cristóbal de las Casas on January 1, 1994, the Zapatistas weren't only making a statement to the Mexican government, they were proclaiming their rejection of the peaceful tactics endorsed by other peasant groups.

Before we look at the rise of these alternative peasant groups, however, we have to look further back at the circumstances that combined in eastern Chiapas to make people receptive to grass roots movements. Several things stand out as unique about eastern Chiapas: the region has a substantial number of religions that are nontraditional for Mexico—Protestant, Evangelical, Mormon, Seventh-Day Adventist, and others—which means it has a population that has already had to challenge the status quo; it has a system of rural networks originally designed to build a sense of religious community among far-flung canyon hamlets but that evolved into a social network grass roots organizers were able to build upon; and, because so many people in eastern Chiapas are refugees from other parts of Mexico, communities tend to be more open, democratic and diverse than Indian villages in the central highlands, which are often tightly organized around ethnicity, Catholicism and *costumbre* (traditional indigenous religious practice).

Protestant Evangelization

The Protestant churches, which made extensive use of lay preachers to proselytize in eastern Chiapas, inadvertently helped lay the groundwork for the grass roots political organizing that came later. When the Catholic Church responded to the challenge of Protestantism in the region, they used lay catechists of their own, helping to create another "network in the jungle."

Protestant and Evangelical churches also offered more participatory and democratic congregations than many of the colonists were accustomed to. Women and children were welcomed and included in religious services, a sharp contrast to the more patriarchal religious practices found in most of the colonists' home towns. Because these new forms of worship were so well received, the Catholic Church in eastern Chiapas began to embrace some of the more democratic features of the Protestant churches. The competition between diverse Protestant, Evangelical, and Catholic churches created an environment in which only a *secular* movement, like that of the Zapatistas, could hope to unite peasants across religious lines and attract both women and men, young and old.

The history of Protestantism in Mexico goes back to the mid-nineteenth century, when the Liberal government invited Presbyterian and other Protestant missionaries into the country to provide what the politicians hoped would be a modernizing counterforce to centuries of Catholicism. In the 1930s, during a period of intense anticlericalism, the government forbade the recitation of mass and, to further curtail the influence of the Catholic Church, allowed Protestant Bible translators to establish themselves in various regions, including Chiapas, where it hoped their work would help advance literacy among the peasants.[5]

Figure 3.1 **The Spread of Protestantism.** Already an established presence in eastern Chiapas by 1960, Protestant religions claimed up to 37% of the populace by 1990 in many townships.

For many years, the Protestants made few converts. As late as the 1970s, one missionary who had lived in the highland Chiapas hamlet of Nauvenchauk for a decade had yet to convert a single person. Around that time, however, the missionaries began to witness a change of heart, especially among the poor, dispossessed, and politically dissident members of Chiapas villages. But those who did convert met with extreme antagonism on the part of village elders in many communities, most notably San Juan Chamula, where leaders ostracized them, confiscated their land, and in some cases burned their houses and forced them to leave town. Many of these refugees eventually settled in eastern Chiapas or became squatters on the fringes of San Cristóbal.[6]

The animosity between "traditional" Catholic Indians and Protestants continues today. Because many Protestant converts forswear alcohol and refuse to pay religious taxes or to participate in traditional religious celebrations, they challenge the established village life. Local political leaders often argue that this lack of conformity justifies expelling Protestants from their villages. Sometimes, nonreligious dissidents are accused of being Protestant as a pretext for ousting them from their homes. Some observers have charged that such expulsions violate Mexico's constitutional guarantees of freedom of religion and the right to property, not to mention internationally recognized human rights.[7] Village traditionalists, however, argue that Mexican civil law has always allowed Indian communities to settle disputes by customary law when felonies are not involved. They claim that expulsions are a time-honored way of dealing with troublesome people. They also say customary law is one way Indian communities preserve their autonomy and argue that forbidding it would be a violation of *their* rights as indigenous peoples. Critics respond that customary law places too much discretion in the hands of village powerholders, or caciques, who often use custom and tradition as an excuse for expelling anyone who challenges their authority.[8]

Many Protestants fled to eastern Chiapas, where the Protestant and Evangelical population comprised between 20 and 51 percent in municipios responding to the 1990 population census. About half of these are Seventh-Day Adventists or Presbyterians; Pentacostals, Evangelicals, and Baptists make up another quarter; there are also Jehovah's Witnesses, Mormons, and half a dozen other churches or sects.[9] While some settlers have brought religions with them, many others have converted to Protestantism after settling in eastern Chiapas, which has a history of evangelicalism, especially along the Guatemalan border.

Why so many different churches? Some of my colleagues who have worked in the area, such as Rosalva Aída Hernández Castillo,[10] suggest that the religions in eastern Chiapas provide homesteaders, who have left their ancestral homes behind, with new ways of forming community. The churches unify people who are trying to establish common ground with neighbors of different origins, ethnic groups, and cultures.

These nontraditional religions may well be more democratic in their practices than their traditional Catholic counterparts in the Chiapas highlands. In the highlands, those who hold religious posts are expected to finance them, and the greater a post's costs, the greater the prestige conferred on those who accept them.[11] In addition to conferring status, completing a term in such a post confers the right to hold forth in public affairs. The costlier the post, the greater the political power. The Protestant, Evangelical, and other nontraditional churches also offer many positions such as elder or deacon that require almost no financial investment. As a result, it is easier for poorer people to become involved, and to attain respected positions. And because religious office is not tied to political power, even those without a church affiliation are able to attain power in civil affairs—something that was once unthinkable in the Chiapas highlands.

The Protestant churches in Chiapas have long attempted to win converts by evangelizing in the native languages of the Maya, a strategy that the Catholic Church had used in the colonial period, but not after Independence, until recently. Markets throughout Chiapas sell cassettes of Protestant and Evangelical hymns sung by indigenous people in their own language and style, spreading the word to the masses. Such grass roots prose-lytizing has not only helped make the nontraditional churches more accessible, but has also helped empower Indians who previously were forced to suffer the indignity of being treated as second-class citizens even in church, where the Catholic priests administered the sacraments only in Spanish. And although Chiapas does not have a high literacy rate compared with the rest of Mexico (69 percent of adults over fifteen years as compared to 87 percent nationally, according to the 1990 census), census statistics show that literacy rates are higher in native-language speaking communities that are Protestant. Even women and girls, whose literacy rates tend to lag far behind those of men, are learning to read.

Recently, while visiting a town where Protestant exiles from Zinacantán have started a new life, I saw Losha, a five-year-old girl, read a passage aloud from a Tzotzil bible. Later in the day, we accompanied Losha and her family to the settlement's Presbyterian church for the afternoon service, one of several services that the family attends each week. An indigenous pastor delivered the sermon. He also spoke of organizing a visit to Sekemtik, back in Zinacantán, to support the Protestants there. What impressed me most was how the new religion had forged a bond of affinity among the residents of this community, how this church had drawn women and children as well as men into a vibrant congregation, creating a space in which people could challenge the boundaries not just of gender and literacy, but of access, through literacy, to formerly impenetrable domains of law and politics.

Protestantism has helped to legitimize literacy, which, in the minds of many Indians, has had negative associations with the repressive laws and policies of the ladino government and, as such, has been viewed historically as a threat to the conventions and *costumbre* that organize the traditional Maya community. But peasants are learning to read and write about their faith in their indigenous languages as well as Spanish, and literacy is coming to be seen as something that is their own, not as something that signifies the ladino world. As literacy is freed from its repressive political context, Mexican politics become more accessible because peasants no longer fear that it will destroy their traditions.

Women especially seem to have found a place in the Protestant churches of eastern Chiapas. They are *always* present at Sunday and weekday services and hold offices in the church, something they were not able to do in the highlands. The move from the highlands was particularly difficult for women, because whereas many men from impoverished towns were accustomed to doing far-flung wage work, many women had never been beyond neighboring towns and were accustomed to being the ones who held their communities together by performing agricultural work while the men were elsewhere. Migrating to the lowlands, women had to leave behind their networks of day-to-day social relations among kin and neighbors. The churches of their new communities have helped them form new bonds to replace those stretched or broken by resettlement.

As women have adapted to their new lives on the frontier, they have also begun to assume new positions in their communities. No one has done a full study of women's roles in eastern Chiapas, but journalists and at least one scholar[12] have noted the active participation of women in the Zapatista movement and its armed forces.

While no one pretends that the Zapatista movement is a women's liberation movement, it does appear that the Zapatistas at least recognize women as an oppressed group. In a February 1, 1994, interview in *Tiempo*, Sub-Comandante Marcos described a Tzotzil woman named Susana, who was responsible for visiting dozens of communities to talk with women about their priorities in order to come up with the Zapatista position on women's rights. At a meeting of the movement's leadership that the Zapatistas refer to as the first battle led by the Zapatista women, she read the following list of demands that Marcos claims was unanimously endorsed.

> We want not to be obliged to marry with he whom we do not want; we want to have the children we choose to, and whom we can care for. We seek the right to hold cargos [religious posts] in the community. We want the right to speak our word and be respected. We want the right to study, and even be truck drivers.[13]

One member of the *Comandancia General*, the steering committee of the Zapatistas, is a Tzotzil woman named Ramona. In an interview with journalists, Ramona urges all women to join the Zapatista movement.

> Because women also are living in difficult situations, women are the most exploited of all, the most oppressed. Why? Because for so many years, for 500 years, they have not had the right to speak, to participate in assemblies, they have no right to education, nor to speak in public, nor to take cargos in their communities. No. The women are completely oppressed and exploited. We get up at 3:00 A.M. to cook corn, and we don't get to rest until the evening after everyone else is asleep. And if there isn't enough food, then we give our tortillas to the children, to our husbands. We [women] demand respect, true respect as Indians. We also have rights . . . and my message to all women who feel exploited, ignored, is take up arms as a Zapatista.[14]

Photo 3.1 **Comandante Ramona.** Ramona, a guerrilla of the Zapatista Army for National Liberation (left) hands a Mexican flag to Sub-comandante Marcos Tuesday, February 22, 1994, in the cathedral of San Cristobal de las Casas, Mexico. Marcos later showed the flag to the media during a press conference and said it was captured by the rebels when they held San Cristobal de las Casas on January 1. (AP Photo/Damian Dovarganes)

Catholic Responses

While we don't yet know the precise makeup of the Zapatista National Liberation Army or who originally organized it, we have many indications about the roles outside organizations played in its early development.

Most observers trace the beginning of the radical peasant movement in Chiapas to 1974, when the state governor asked Bishop Samuel Ruiz to organize an Indigenous Congress commemorating the birth of Fray Bartolomé de las Casas, the sixteenth-century champion of Indian rights. The purpose of this congress was twofold. On one hand, the Catholic Church, exercising what it called its "preferential option for the poor," wanted to give voice to the sufferings of Indians; the government, on the other hand, wanted to create a more populist image after brutally repressing the student movement of the late 1960s.

Before 1974, the Catholic Church had already begun extensive grass roots evangelizing in eastern Chiapas, in part to ward off the advance of Protestantism. When asked to help prepare for the Congress, church planners made use of their evangelical networks in the region, which were divided into several districts according to the principal indigenous languages: Chol, Tojolabal, Tzeltal, and Tzotzil. Traveling catechists organized groups of neighboring parishes into evangelical districts and visited them frequently, assembling parishioners each month in a different town, and staying in parishioners' homes. In addition to translating sermons and books of the Bible into indigenous languages, the catechists, many indigenous people themselves, talked about Fray Bartolomé de las Casas and his struggle for Indian rights. They asked indigenous people to think about their current circumstances and difficulties and to delegate members of their communities to come to the Congress and talk about their hopes, desires, and priorities for the future.

It is important to note that the Indigenous Congress (and the grass roots evangelizing in indigenous languages that was done by both the Catholic and the Protestant churches) took place at a time when peasants and Indians were held in disregard not just by average citizens but by the intelligentsia as well. Even several strands of Marxist political thought derided ethnicity as "false consciousness," exerting a strong influence over intellectuals who held high positions even in Indianist-oriented government organizations such as PRODESCH, the Socioeconomic Development Program for the Highlands of Chiapas. (PRODESCH was set up in 1970 to coordinate state, federal, and international development efforts in Chiapas.) Because ethnic identity was thought to keep Indians from contributing to development, PRODESCH had abrogated earlier National Indianist Institute efforts to promote bilingual education for Indians. Although PRODESCH worked through indigenous agents, the agency did not hesitate to make decisions for Indians, for example by imposing its own candidates for municipal office on Indian townships.

The Indigenous Congress, thus, was unprecedented in the history of Chiapas, for it was the first official meeting of Indians not convened for the government to tell Indians what to do. Indigenous people had been convened before, but usually by

Indianist agencies that wanted indigenous people to embrace policies or programs designed by government planners. The Indigenous Congress of 1974, on the other hand, was a grass roots convention for Indians and by Indians and offered a chance for indigenous people to voice their own solutions to the problems that confronted them. Unlike the government-sponsored peasant and indigenous organizations, which are organized from the top down, the congress provided a model of bottom-up organizing upon which independent peasant organizations subsequently drew.

During the Indigenous Congress, the delegates talked about the same bread and butter issues the Zapatistas have: land, food, education, and health. The following passages, the first from the Indigenous Congress and the second, issued twenty years later in the early days of the Zapatista uprising, are almost identical. The demands have remained constant for the past two decades.

-From the 1974 Indigenous Congress:[15]

> *On land:* We have problems with ranchers who invade our lands . . . . We need land, we don't have enough of it, so we have to rent it, or go away to work. The lands we have been given are infertile. We need to be taught our rights under the Agrarian Laws.
>
> *On health:* Doctors are concentrated in the cities and never attend in the countryside . . . . The programs of public health are not realistic . . . . We are sold bad out-of-date medicine that is useless . . . . Merchants are making a business out of selling false medicine, or by selling [government] medicines that are supposed to be free.[16]
>
> *On services:* We pay taxes, but we don't receive even basic services such as running water.
>
> *On food:* We all suffer from malnutrition and poverty, because of lack of land.
>
> *On education:* The education system is very poor and does not serve to improve our communities.
>
> *On work:* We are paid very unfair salaries and are forced to work from sunrise to sunset.
>
> *On commerce:* Peasants and Indians work hard but are always exploited. We have to sell our products cheap, but whatever we buy is expensive. For us, merchants and middlemen are like a plague of locusts.

On malnutrition: Our suffering is due to lack of nutrition, poverty, and lack of land.

-From the Zapatistas' 34-point agenda for negotiation in 1994:[17]

8. Land is for the Indians and peasants who work it, not for the large landlords. We demand that the copious lands in the hands of ranchers, foreign and national landlords, and other non-peasants be turned over to our communities, which totally lack land . . . .

9. We ask for hospitals in the municipal centers provisioned with enough medicine to attend patients, and for rural clinics staffed with trained and properly paid health agents . . . . .

11. We demand the construction of housing . . . with basic services such as electricity, water, plumbing, telephones . . . , and such advantages as televisions, stoves, refrigerators, washing machines, etc . . . .

12. We demand an end to illiteracy among the indigenous communities, and for this we need better primary and secondary schools with free textbooks and university-trained teachers who are ready to serve the people, and not just the rich . . . .

18. We demand dignified and fairly paid work for all rural and urban workers . . . .

19. We ask for fair prices for our farm products and markets where we can freely sell and buy without being at the mercy of *coyotes* [exploitative middlemen] . . . .

21. Let there be an end to hunger and malnutrition, which have caused the deaths of thousands of our rural and urban brothers.

The work of the 1974 Indigenous Congress did not cease with the congress itself—catechists took its lessons back to indigenous communities in the various districts. They screened a film that had been made about the congress and taught courses in native languages on the history of Mexico and Chiapas, political economy, and Mexican commerce. Following the organizing strategy used to prepare for the congress, the catechists continued to meet with indigenous representatives from the various districts, each time in a different place, to build a base for popular participation, including that of women and children.[18]

In the end, however, the catechists' efforts met with the limitations of their association with the Catholic Church in a landscape of religious pluralism. However much the Catholic Church hoped to speak with a universal voice, it could not do so persuasively while attempting to win people away from other religions. Only a truly secular movement appealing broadly to pluralism and democracy could hope to galvanize the indigenous and peasant community across its religious diversity. By 1978, a movement known as Popular Politics (*Política Popular*), began to do just that, gradually displacing the catechists from their central role in organizing eastern Chiapas.

Although the role of the Church in fomenting revolution remains difficult to assess, it is clear that most later independent peasant organizing in Chiapas drew lessons and inspiration, and in some cases their actual beginnings, from the 1974 congress.

In a September 13, 1993, interview in *Proceso*, Mardonio Morales says, "It [radical peasant organizing] all started shortly after the Indigenous Congress of 1974." The Zapatistas, not quite as bluntly, also point to 1974 as the starting point for radical agitation.

> Years have passed, since about 1974, when we began trying to get land, dwellings, roads, rural clinics, but without any success. The only response was trickery and false promises.[19]

Morales said some priests did go underground to help bring about revolution, but the Zapatistas are not nearly as forthcoming. In communiques published in *Tiempo* on January 12 and 19, 1994, the Zapatistas denied the influence of outsiders and refuted claims that radical Catholic priests or catechists had inspired them to take up arms.

> The EZLN does not have any foreigners in its ranks, and has not received support or advice from revolutionary movements of other countries or other governments . . . .We have never had ties with the Salvadoran FMLN, nor with the URGN of Guatemala, nor with any armed movement of any part of the world. We learned our tactics from Mexican history itself, from Hidalgo, Morelos, Guerrero, Mina, from the resistance to the Yankee invasion of 1846–1847, and from popular resistance to the French intervention, from the heroic deeds of Villa and Zapata and from the long history of indigenous resistance in our country.

> We have no links to Catholic religious authorities, nor with those of any other creed . . . Among the ranks, the majority are Catholic, but there are also other creeds and religions.[20]

And

> We are not religious, nor are we against religion. We respect
> beliefs, but each one of us is in the battle for our poverty.
> There are catechists among us, also *sabáticos* (Seventh-Day
> Adventists).[21]

Peasant Organizations

The 1974 Indigenous Congress had two important consequences for peasant and indigenous organizing in Chiapas. First,
by convening indigenous groups from different parts of the state,
the congress helped develop an awareness of shared problems
across ethnic lines. It established channels for ongoing communication and helped build bridges between groups that would later
serve to organize alliances. Second, the congress presented nonindigenous organizers and activists, including teachers and technical advisors, with incontrovertible proof that Indians, even
monolingual speakers of different Mayan languages with distinct
ethnicities and cultural identities, could organize and share awareness of one another's circumstances.

For years preceding the Congress, indigenous and other peasants had been the topic of much debate among Mexico's Left.
Many intellectuals[22] denied the political potential of the country's
indigenous peoples and claimed that they were not worth organizing because they represented an anachronistic, regressive sector of
society that impeded the development of the proletarian class consciousness needed to overthrow capitalism. These scholars,
steeped in the tenets of classical Marxism, believed that revolution
could only come from a wage-earning working class in a fully
developed capitalist society. They rejected the Maoist idea that
peasants in a precapitalist society were capable of progressive political action that could lead to the overthrow of the state. They
argued that peasant agitation for land reform was not something
the Left should support because peasants' inherently inefficient
production held back the development of the agrarian sector and,
thus, of capitalism. They also believed that Indians were nothing
more than pawns of the bourgeois state, easily coopted as buffers
against development of rural proletarians, their ethnicity and culture nothing more than a false consciousness abetted by the
Mexican government's Indianist programs. After the Cuban

Revolution, the failure of *Che Guevarismo*—the theory that leaders such as Ernesto "Che" Guevara could appear on the peasant or indigenous scene and ignite latent revolutionary potential—only seemed to further prove the reactionary character of the peasantry.

Other intellectuals on the Left vehemently rejected this characterization of the peasantry. Arturo Warman, author of *We Come to Object: The Peasants of Morelos and the National State*, argued that peasant production, spurred by Lázaro Cárdenas's agrarian reform in the 1930s, had been indispensable to the development of Mexico's urban economy by providing cheap food and thus enabling industry to keep wages low. Alain de Janvry, writing about agrarian reform throughout Latin America in *The Agrarian Question*, pointed out that peasants should be considered semiproletarians because, while they grow food in the countryside, they also sell labor as occasional workers in the city. Other analysts[23] argued that peasants, in their quest for land, were not so different from workers striking for better work conditions in the field or the factory, and that the seeming inefficiency of peasant production was actually a result of middlemen and power holders in the countryside, who robbed them of fair returns by buying corn and beans from them cheaply while selling needed merchandise to them dearly, or by charging usurious interest to peasants who needed loans. If anything, these scholars argued, peasants needed the support of the Left in gaining access to land and assistance in obtaining fair markets and reasonable credits.

Needless to say, the impact of the Indigenous Congress of 1974 was watched closely by intellectuals on both sides of the debate. The success of the congress, and the informal programs—such as the lessons in political economy, commerce, and Mexican history that Indians in the Selva Lacandona requested and received from Catholic catechists in the months following the congress—seemed to underscore both the sophistication and the progressive potential of indigenous peoples. That these courses were taught in the countryside, in Tzeltal, served even further to demonstrate the viability of grass roots education in what had previously been perceived as a backward and conservative sector of society. Activists in other parts of the country busy developing nongovernmental independent popular organizations took note of the congress's accomplishments and many urban intellectuals were forced to reform their views of the peasantry.

The national government, meanwhile, hoping to capitalize on the effervescence of the Congress and coopt its leaders, convoked its own National Congress of Indian Pueblos in 1975 at Pátzcuaro, Michoacán (the site of the First Interamerican Indian Congress that my grandfather, John Collier, attended in 1940 as U.S. Commissioner of Indian Affairs). Both developments—the lessons that came out of the Church-sponsored Indigenous Congress of 1974 and the government-sponsored congress a year later—drew the indigenous peasants of Chiapas into the national arena. This opened Chiapas to important new currents of organizing and politics, just at the time when federally sponsored colonization was sending peasants from central and northern Mexico to homestead in eastern Chiapas.

During the 1970s, the federal government entered into a rivalry with leftist movements for control of worker and peasant organizations. During the 1970–76 presidency of Luis Echeverría, the state used populism, agrarian reform, and colonization to draw some peasants into the fold of the ruling party. José López Portillo, in the 1976–82 presidency that followed, poured money from the oil boom into local programs to win support. At the same time, independent organizers were attempting to win support from peasants frustrated with the government's lack of action on land reform petitions. The repression of the student movement in 1968 had persuaded Mexico's Left to avoid direct political confrontation with the state by pressing for reforms through legal channels. The independent organizations emerging at the time tended to parallel those of the government and competed with them for membership while challenging the government to embrace more radical concerns. Eventually, this competition led to friction not just between government authorities and political organizers, but between independently organized peasants and government-affiliated peasants who ended up challenging each other for the same pieces of land (as we noted in the previous chapter) or the same credits.

The 1970s also marked the beginning of a new way of thinking about peasants and Indians. For decades, Mexican intellectuals had considered the "Indian question" as distinct from the "peasant question." And the government, accordingly, assumed that each group had its own distinct—and not necessarily overlapping—interests. The government and ruling party treated peasants as a social sector (*sector social*)—comparable to but distinct from labor, industry, or commerce. The social sector was subsidized as such and allocated its own channel of political access within the ruling party through the National Peasant Confederation (CNC). Peasants, labor, and Indians each had their own, separate PRI-sponsored organization: for peasants, the National Peasant Confederation (CNC); for labor, the Confederation of Mexican Workers (CTM); and for Indians, the National Indianist Institute (INI) and state-level departments of Indian affairs. The CNC and CTM were organizations within the PRI and served both to give members access to and representation within the ruling party leadership and as a channel for the government to reach out to constituents. The INI was responsible for Indianist programs of development. Despite the fact that most Indians were also peasants and the two groups had many areas of shared interest and concern—how to raise better crops, how to improve marginal land, how to gain access to more land, get better prices for crops and obtain credit, for example—no links were made between these organizations. In fact, before the 1970s, even Indians whose communities held land under agrarian reform weren't accepted into the CNC.

But by the 1970s, intellectuals such as André Gunder Frank and Rodolfo Stavenhagen had begun to analyze the Indian *and* peasant questions together as part and parcel of Mexico's agrarian class structure.

Challenges to the Government

Three distinct independent organizing movements arose in Chiapas in the 1970s and 1980s. One, typified by the Emiliano Zapata Peasant Organization (OCEZ) focused primarily on land reform and was centered initially in the Grijalva River valley town of Venustiano Carranza, where conflict between ranchers and peasants that had brewed for years flared after the government tried to relocate Angostura dam floodplain settlements there. OCEZ struggled to prevent evictions and relocations of ejidos and to help peasants gain title to contested lands. The second movement, based in northern Chiapas in the area around Simojovel, operated on the premise that peasants were part of a rural proletariat that should be organized into labor unions. The Independent Confederation of Agricultural Workers and Indians (CIOAC) took the lead in this region by organizing resident workers, who were notoriously underpaid and mistreated, to sue ranchers under federal labor laws for back wages and improved working conditions. The third type of organizing focused on making credits available to small producers, and drew strength from the Popular Politics (PP), a Maoist student movement led by a Mexico City economics professor. Although the PP was at the outset primarily a northern Mexican movement, many students involved in the PP eventually came to eastern Chiapas to work among the people who lived in impoverished frontier communities.

Land-focused organizing arrived in Chiapas after the 1975 National Indigenous Congress that the government convoked in Pátzcuaro, Michoacán. Its development illustrates the rivalry between government and independent organizations at the national level that reverberated in peasant organizing in Chiapas. The Pátzcuaro congress brought together indigenous representatives from throughout the country, including Chiapas. After the congress, the government established a National Council of Indian Pueblos (CNPI) to guide development of programs discussed at the congress. At first, the government controlled the council and used it to fund regional programs, such as those of bilingual cultural agents in Oaxaca. But by 1979, when the council's leadership fell into the hands of independent organizers, many of whom were committed to agitating for agrarian reform, the government closed the council down. The independents reorganized it as the *Plan de Ayala* National Coordinating Committee (CNPA), named after the 1911 *Plan de Ayala* proclamation setting forth Emiliano Zapata's proposal to expropriate lands, woods, and water that had been usurped from peasants by landlords and politicians.[24]

The CNPA forged a broad alliance of peasant groups from throughout Mexico, including Chiapas, to demand agrarian reform under the banner of Emiliano Zapata. The CNPA also allied itself with another powerful independent union, that of teachers who had split off from the government-controlled national teachers' union. Together, the two independent organizations led a nationwide mass march on Mexico City on May 12,

1981, to demand the release of political prisoners and the resolution of 315 pending land claims. They organized a second demonstration in June 1982, shortly before their fifth national congress, held in Venustiano Carranza, Chiapas. As a result, Venustiano Carranza became the focal point in Chiapas for long-lasting statewide linkages among the region's CNPA affiliates, who established the OCEZ as a network of independent peasant organizations struggling for agrarian reform in Chiapas, often in alliance with the state's independent teachers movement.[25] Trenchantly opposed to the ruling party's national peasant union, OCEZ spread Zapatista ideology throughout Chiapas during the 1980s.[26]

The second influential current of independent organizing that entered Chiapas from the national arena in the late 1970s focused on labor. The CIOAC was established in 1975 in affiliation with Mexican communists and socialists; its leaders urged the Left to consider peasants as proletarians, pointing out that at the turn of the century, most of Mexico's rural poor had worked as laborers in the developing capitalist agriculture of the period. Should their descendants be considered peasants just because Mexico's agrarian reform had given them some land? After all, many peasants had to hire themselves out as field hands because they still didn't have enough land on which to make a living. And on ranches that had escaped expropriation under agrarian reform, thousands of resident workers lived in poverty. CIOAC argued that all these rural poor should be considered rural proletarians and incorporated into the proletarian workers' movement.[27]

CIOAC arrived on the scene in northern Chiapas in 1977 and began to use federal labor laws as a basis for demanding agrarian reform on behalf of the resident workers on coffee estates in the region of Simojovel. CIOAC organizers argued that ranch owners violated minimum wage and fair labor standards by paying resident workers only token wages and/or giving them marginal plots on which to live and cultivate in exchange for three days' labor per week. CIOAC helped resident workers organize to sue ranch owners in the Simojovel area for back wages—and for the ranches themselves when back wages exceeded the value of a given plantation. In effect, CIOAC opened up a channel for resident workers to claim land *outside* of the conventional application of Mexico's agrarian reform.

Figure 3.2 **Independent Organizations in Chiapas.** Areas of influence in the 1980s.

This tactic developed at a time when the Mexican government was flush with petrodollars, which the ruling party channeled through state governments to finance development in order to calm dissent. With this goal in mind, Juan Sabines, governor of Chiapas, decided in 1980 to buy out ranches in Simojovel and nearby areas and to offer them for sale to resident workers, financed by CIOAC claims for back pay or by bank loans. For a time, this tactic propelled CIOAC to the forefront of independent peasant organizing in Chiapas. But it also opened CIOAC to criticism, not only from factions within the OCEZ for whom the resort to federal labor laws as a basis for land claims seemed to bypass and thus threaten the agrarian reform laws, but also from independent groups who interpreted the buy out of lands as selling out or compromising with the ruling party.[28]

By far the most powerful current of independent organizing in eastern Chiapas during the 1970s focused on credits and markets and grew out of a political current that began in northern Mexico as the Popular Politics and organized by establishing *ejido* unions as credit and marketing organizations. This movement grew out of a faction of the student movement that decided, after 1968, to live and work with the masses to help them organize in a nonviolent struggle for socialism. A Mexican National Autonomous University economist, Adolfo Orive Berlinguer, had argued in a 1968 pamphlet "*Hacia una política popular*" ("Towards a Politics of the People"), that the masses had the capacity to organize at the grass roots, and that the role of theorists and analysts was to help the masses realize their capabilities. An important tenet was to organize from the ground up, with leadership authorized from below— rather than from above. The goal of organizing was to help empower people to become the protagonists of their own destinies without directly challenging the government.

Inspired by Orive and anxious to put his ideas to work, former students turned to the poor in the urban neighborhoods and rural communities of central and northern Mexico, and to the rank and file of teacher's and worker's unions, to build movements that would seek improved living and working conditions for people who had previously been ignored by society. In its rural efforts, the movement met with particular success in collective *ejidos* among the Yaqui and Mayo Indians of Sinaloa and Sonora[29] and by establishing member-run credit and marketing organizations to circumvent exploitation by merchants, middlemen, and usurers. Adherents of the PP, and of the Proletarian Line (LP), in which the PP joined teachers, metalworkers, and telephone workers organizing in the north, also practiced what they called "two-faced" politics of "pretexts and objectives." Unlike some more radical groups, which were staunchly against any sort of compromise with the government, the PP advocated interactions with the government that might appear to be compromises but which, in fact, furthered the PP's objectives and could be justified as a means to an end. This tactic was often interpreted by other peasant groups as selling out.

Of all the independent movements, Popular Politics was the most similar in theory and practice to Catholic liberation theology, which explains why PP advocates from the north appeared on the scene both during and in the wake of the 1974 Indigenous Congress in San Cristóbal to offer assistance to catechists organizing and educating peasants and Indians in eastern Chiapas. Orive is said to have offered his personal services to the Church, although just what relationship developed between the catechists and the "northerners" isn't clear because some members of the Church deny any involvement with Orive or radical politics. Under Mexican law, the Church must not step over an imaginary line that separates social service and humanitarian advocacy from politics. Yet in some instances the Church may have blurred that line by giving the northerners access to rural assemblies and meetings immediately *after* the catechists had their say.

In an interview with *Proceso* several months before the Zapatista uprising, Mardonio Morales, who served in the Selva Lacandona for more than thirty years, recalled what he said was the first meeting between Orive and Church activists two decades earlier.

> [Orive said] "I have come to make you an offer. You take charge of pastoral matters and we will handle political organization. You have the communities in your hands; in this way we can complete our work."
>
> Afterward, he left so that we could discuss it. In general, we thought it would be dishonest to turn the communities over to people who, though apparently very well intentioned, were outsiders. It was a kind of agreement between elites . . . . We thought that it was not a good idea to ally ourselves with them, that if they wanted to come in and work in the communities, we would not close the doors, but neither would we turn the communities over to them. Therefore, there was no deal. Mr. Orive was informed and we severed our ties. We never heard from him again.[30]

However, Morales told *Proceso* that some members of the Church and some secular missionaries secretly established ties with Orive and the northerners, allowing PP organizers to talk to groups after the catechizers had concluded their meetings in the years following the 1974 Congress. At first, Morales is quoted as saying, the northerners seemed to make some concrete improvements in the lives of impoverished eastern Chiapas residents.

> They worked with great sacrifice and devotion, these men and women from Torreón. Thus, they quickly founded the Quiptic ta Lecoptusel, the Union of Unions, then the ARICS— in short, a number of very strong, effective organizations. All indications were that they were on the ascendant.[31]

Within a few years of the 1974 Indigenous Congress, the north-erners had displaced the Catholic organizers of the Congress as the dominant intellectual force behind eastern Chiapas's first large coalitions of settlers, formed to obtain credits for peasants. The Quiptik ta Lekubtesel (United for Our Improvement) union gal-vanized 26 communities within the Montes Azul bioreserve and the San Quintín valley of Ocosingo to resist government reloca-tion. In the Selva Lacandona and Las Margaritas, agitation for land and against relocation were used to win a variety of conces-sions from the government, including credits for small farmers[32] and assistance marketing crops.

One concession, won in 1979, was to have INMECAFE, the Mexican Coffee Institute, absorb the considerable cost of trans-porting coffee produced by member communities in eastern Chiapas to national markets. A second concession, won from Chiapas governor Juan Sabines in September 1980, was to allow the separate independent coalitions to join together in one overar-ching Union of Unions, which would administer production cred-its and productivity incentives sponsored by the federal government to revive Mexico's production of basic foods. The Union of Unions quickly expanded to include affiliates in the cen-tral highlands of Chiapas and along the Guatemalan border. One year later, from October 12–14, 1981, the Union of Unions mobi-lized a march and sit-down strike of some 3,000 peasants in Tuxtla Gutiérrez to demand reversal of the eviction orders for the twenty-six communities affected by the Montes Azul bioreserve. Indepen-dent teacher's, student's, and worker's groups accompanied them. In Mexico City, the Independent Worker's Union coordinated a sympathy march in support of the Union of Union's objectives.[33]

By the mid-1980s, the three movements—land-based, labor-based, and credit-based—had spread through the historically undeveloped half of Chiapas from the region around Simojovel to the Selva Lacandona. The movements crossed over one another's original bases of power, sometimes in competition and sometimes in alliance, and established networks of communication across a vast landscape.

The Union of Unions, for example, armed with independent credits and special market access after forming a pact with Chiapas Governor Juan Sabines at Bajucú (Las Margaritas) in 1980, quickly became an organizing force in the Simojovel region some one hundred miles to the northwest. There, in the heartland of CIOAC's support, the Union of Unions helped resident workers and Tzotzil colonists band together to take over ranches such as Cucalvitz. Using a combination of violence, threats, and finally bank credits, Tzotzil Indians purchased this ranch, renaming it *Kipaltik,* or Our Union. They began mixed production of milpa, cattle, and coffee as a collective. When the time came to undertake the first coffee harvests, one of the organizers of the Kipaltik collective, a man who had participated in the Bajucú pact with Governor Sabines in 1980, recruited compatriots (through his network of ties to distant Las Margaritas) to help with the harvest.[34]

The CIOAC and OCEZ began, during the 1980s, to cooperate in militant organizing. Initially they had diverged over the discrepancy between OCEZ's emphasis on using the agrarian code as a basis for militancy and CIOAC's emphasis on federal labor laws. But they began to collaborate in one another's demonstrations and marches, developing networks of mutual support through which protestors could be mobilized quickly to support their organizations' causes. CIOAC and OCEZ also began to expand their activities out of their respective heartlands (northern Chiapas in the area around Simojovel; Venustiano Carranza on the western fringe of the central Grijalva River valley) and into the eastern Chiapas regions once predominantly the domain of the Popular Politics movement and the Union of Unions. By the end of the 1980s, CIOAC and OCEZ had shifted their most militant activity to the Las Margaritas and Ocosingo areas, respectively, making inroads in the heartland of the Union of Unions (UU).

Disillusionment and Disagreement

What caused those who now support the Zapatistas to lose faith in the alternative peasant groups and in peaceful forms of resistance?

Some of the Zapatistas' most bitter critiques have been directed at leaders of independent movements or organizations who they say have sold out to the ruling party and betrayed their broader constituencies. CIOAC had received some such criticism from the OCEZ during the early 1980s when CIOAC accepted Chiapas governor Juan Sabines's policy of buying out ranches in northern

Chiapas and offering them to resident workers. The Union of Unions opened itself to similar criticism by agreeing to tone down militancy in exchange for legal recognition, marketing arrangements with the Mexican Coffee Institute, and support for its independent credit union.

The ARIC Union of Unions split from the Union of Unions (UU) shortly after 1980 to protest the UU's arrangements with the state governor to form its credit union. In 1989, it seemed itself to have compromised with the government when Salinas de Gortari, in the first days of his presidency, recognized the land claims of the twenty-six ARIC communities settled within the Montes Azul bioreserve and granted ARIC control of a network of subsidized food outlets in the Cañadas region of Las Margaritas, close to the clandestine headquarters of the EZLN. Sub-Comandante Marcos has been outspoken in his disapproval of this arrangement, suggesting that in return for money, ARIC leaders agreed to promote support for the ruling party amongst their followers. In a 1994 statement printed in *Tiempo*, he argued:

> [F]rankly, . . . there are big lies being woven against us with the approval of the army and the evil government. And complicit in those lies are authorities and advisors of the ARIC-Union of Unions, who sold out when the supreme government and their armed forces offered food outlets and money . . . . Some . . . of the authorities in the ARIC-Union of Unions and its advisors have sold out and are [government] accomplices. Why? Are they not also poor Indians? The answer, brothers, is that . . . everyone knows that the majority of the aid that the federal government sent over the past several years to alleviate the hardships of life in our pueblos stayed in their hands. These men fear that their theft will be discovered, as well as their complicity with state and municipal authorities against their brothers of race and blood. Brothers, turn away from those traitors, don't listen to them when they come with their "politics of two faces" to trick others and obtain personal benefits.[35]

In what seemed like a blatant attempt to buy votes for the August 1994 presidential election, the government in May granted almost 6 million new pesos (approximately 1.8 million U.S. dollars) in credits to ARIC and other Union of Unions subsidiaries,[36] lending credence to Marcos's accusation that the ARIC has compromised its principles for money.

I think that the Zapatista rebellion builds upon deep disillusion with both the national state and the independent peasant organizations. In 1974, the Indigenous Congress had inspired the vision that indigenous and nonindigenous peasants could be forged into an alliance with progressive currents from other parts of the country to mobilize for change within the framework of the law. But the 1982 debt crisis, the elimination of government subsidies, Salinas de Gortari's determination to end agrarian reform, and continuing repression, made doing so seem less and less possible. In a country with little money in a world that demands modernization, peasants have little leverage. When independent peasant organizations have won concessions from the government, they have paid dearly for them by losing credibility with their wider constituencies. Worse, the leaders of some organizations have agreed to compromises that benefit few peasants at the expense of many others. Each such pact has made it seem less likely that the disenfranchised will ever have their day in court. By taking up arms, the EZLN has attempted to remove the peasants' struggle from the arena of corrupt Mexican law and politics.

I believe, above all, that the Zapatistas have rendered judgement against the fundamental tactic of two decades of independent organizing—that of seeking change through legal channels. Time and again, the national state has shown its capacity to exercise the law as a tool for power, selectively and illegitimately, to thwart the revindication of indigenous, peasant, and worker demands.

Every independent movement has experienced repression, either directly from the state's judicial police and military or at the hands of private ranchers' hired gunmen and thugs, who are tolerated and sometimes even abetted by the state. On July 15, 1980, soldiers and ranchers in police uniforms drove over seven hundred resident workers and family members from the ranch that they claimed at Wolonchón (Sitalá), left twelve dead and many wounded, and chased the survivors into the mountains. Ranchers and their henchmen burned and razed peasant settlements to destroy the nucleus of population legally required as the basis of a land claim. During a six month period between July and December 1982, independent organizers and the groups they represented in Chiapas experienced five assassinations, violent evictions from two ranches, the destruction of an entire peasant town, and fifty-nine kidnappings. Sometimes peasants acted against other peasants in such incidents, but in the majority (some 80 percent) of cases of repression in Chiapas reported in the press between 1974 and 1987, ranchers (and their gunmen) and public authorities (judicial and security police of the state or federal government or the army) perpetrated the acts of violence against peasants.[37]

If anything, repression escalated in Chiapas after 1982 under the heavy hand of Governor Absalón Castellanos Domínguez, the retired army general later kidnapped by the EZLN from his ranch near Las Margaritas on January 1, 1994. Peasant leaders were assassinated, leaving groups with the memory of their lost heros, men such as "Bartolomé Martínez Villatoro, Miguel de la Cruz, Alfredo Morales, José Solís, Andulio Gálvez and so many others" who "fell to the bullets of landlords' pistoleros and the state's own police forces."[38] Under the pretext of controlling drug trafficking, judicial police kept up constant repressive vigilance—in one case that I know of personally, "disappeared" a young man in 1989 because they claimed they found wild poppy growing in his flower gardens. After two weeks during which his family could not even find out where their son was being held, he reappeared, toothless and bruised from the beatings he had received in interrogation. Such ongoing abuses of legally instituted power in Chiapas and elsewhere in Mexico have been documented by Americas Watch and other human rights groups,[39] and underscore the Zapatista contention that

> Constitutional laws have not been complied with by those who govern the country, while, on the contrary, we peasants and Indians are made to pay for the tiniest error, under the full weight of the laws drawn up by those who are the first to violate them.[40]

As for elections, the ruling party did everything it could in 1988 to thwart the Cardenista National Democratic Front (FDN), which united the left with dissidents who had split off from the PRI. In 1988, for the first time in years, independent groups decided to participate in electoral politics, but to little avail. In Las Margaritas—to take just one of hundreds of examples— Cardenistas charged in June 1988 that PRI municipal authorities had moved polling places out of the settlements known to have

FDN sympathizers, had failed to register eight hundred Cardenistas, and had doctored voting lists in PRI-controlled settlements by registering the voters there up to six or seven times. In addition, thousands of Cardenista voter identification cards had been stolen in transit from Ocosingo to Las Margaritas.[41] Official election results strained credulity, reporting overwhelming PRI majorities in the rural regions of eastern Chiapas where the Cardenistas were strongest.

> Why is it that the PRI always wins so many votes in Chiapas, 90 percent of the vote, or more? It's because of fraud . . . . No one can tell us, "Well, you should have tried elections . . . ." We did everything legal that we could so far as elections and organizations were concerned, and to no avail.[42]

Once again, the government had closed off a channel of legal recourse, justifying an armed rebellion to force Salinas's resignation and to reform the democratic process.

The Zapatistas, moreover, held the national state responsible for corrupting public officials by enabling them to use Indians, peasants, and the working class poor as rungs on the ladder to power, to be dispensed with or simply forgotten once politicians had attained important positions.

> It has always been easy for the politicians to use us Indians as a step on the ladder for them to climb to power, and once there in power, in their cabinet, they forget about us.[43]

> All of them are to blame, from the highest federal officials to the last of the corrupt "indigenous" leaders, the governor that was not elected by people of Chiapas, the municipal presidents, more concerned with [public] works of adornment and with close ties to the grandees than with governing for their own people, as well as all the other functionaries, who withheld health, education, services, work, justice, food, and above all respect and dignity.[44]

I cannot but wonder whether other leftists of Marcos's generation and background are included in this indictment for having taken up government positions. Arturo Warman, whose *"We Come to Object"* was a scathing critique of Mexico's use of agrarian policy to exploit the peasants, became director of Mexico's Nationalist Indianist Institute (INI) under Salinas, helped formulate the "reform" of Article 27 of the Constitution and the

Agrarian Code, and is now Public Attorney for Agrarian Affairs. Gustavo Gordillo, an activist in Popular Politics (PP) in earlier years and, like Warman, a harsh critic of the corruption in Mexican agrarian policy, also became an advisor to Salinas as Subsecretary of Agrarian Reform and formulated proposals for restructuring the agrarian reform,[45] many of which have been incorporated into the new Agrarian Code.[46] Even Adolfo Orive Berlinguer, the ideologue of Popular Politics, has held office in Salinas's National Solidarity Program. There are many others in government positions whom Marcos and his compatriots may be indicting as sellouts.

The Growth of the Guerilla Movement

Although widespread fraud in the 1988 elections may have helped radicalize more segments of society, the Zapatistas had apparently given up on using legal means to change the system long before the elections debacle that brought Salinas de Gortari to power.

According to Major Mario of the EZLN, the clandestine Zapatista army had its inception on November 16, 1983, when six idealists from Mexico's north arrived to join forces with dissident peasants and Indians in a movement that immediately went underground to begin military and political organizing. Mario was a boy at the time, but he especially remembers one of the six, a charismatic and committed man who was accidentally shot and killed in troop exercises, and whom the Zapatistas commemorate with their left-hand salute to the flag because the man was left-handed.[47] Sub-Comandante Marcos, who was one of the six, says of that moment,

> it was when we arrived that the military question began. There was no military organization before I arrived, we initiated it. We came from a national context similar in process to what is happening now [1994] in the state. Avenues for political action were closing down, and the gap was growing between the two Mexicos that are, in reality three: Mexico of the powerful; Mexico of those who aspire to power; and the Mexico of those who nobody cares about. In Chiapas, these are the Indians. So we decided that something had to be done.[48]

The early 1980s were a time of economic crisis in Mexico. In the last months of the López Portillo presidency in 1982, oil prices

collapsed and the stability of the world banking system was threatened because of Mexico's sudden inability to service its huge international debt. The international financial community forced
Mexico to make huge cuts in federal expenditures, sharply devalue
the peso, slash wages, and remove subsidies for urban and rural
poor. The illusions of petrodollar development shattered and with
them, no doubt, the expectation that independent organizations
could gain economic concessions from the state. On Mexico's
southern border, refugees from Guatemala's war fled into Mexico,
pursued by the Guatemalan military, and bringing the Mexican
military onto the scene to control refugees in what many colonists
of the region believed were joint Guatemalan/Mexican military
maneuvers to repress the colonists as well. Meanwhile, Zoque
Indians and peasants fleeing the northern Chiapas region devastated by ash from the April 1982 eruption of the Chichonal volcano
were swelling the flow of colonists into the south. Avenues for political action were indeed closing down, the divide between the powerful and the poor was growing, and frontier Chiapas was becoming
a dumping ground for both Guatemalan and Mexican refugees.

Retreating into the jungle, the six northern idealists and their
peasant and indigenous compatriots began a process of mutual
education. The northerners had to learn how to survive in the
rugged backlands. "The Lacandón jungle, for a ladino, is the worst
thing that can happen to you, worse than watching '24 Hours' [a
program of Mexico's *Televisa* network]," recounts Marcos. "We
came here in a process of apprenticeship. The comrades taught me
what they know about the mountains, and I taught them what I
know . . . . It was the Indians who taught us how to get around
here, to live in the mountains, to hunt, and then we gradually
began to study weapons. That's how the EZLN arose, but at first
it was sheerly a struggle to survive, to learn how to live in the
mountains, make the mountains accept us."[49]

One task for the movement was to develop a political organization that could extend to embrace new constituencies. Following
the precepts of Popular Politics, like those of Catholic and independent organizers in eastern Chiapas, political organizing was
put entirely into the hands of the movement's indigenous base,
in part because of a recognition that the indigenous people of
the region would never follow a nonindigenous leadership. In

principle, the EZLN organized its leadership through upward the delegation of representation within the ethnic regions that had been established by the 1974 Congress. Clearly, the organization did not represent all peoples within various ethnicities, but it did explicitly draw its legitimacy from followers recruited among all ethnicities. It was in the name of this popular base that the EZLN's leadership, the Committee of Clandestine Indigenous Revolution (CCRI), declared war on January 1, 1994, and it was to this base that it submitted the tentative March 2 peace accords, for what proved, on June 12, to be rejection.

Mardonio Morales recalled the period when he told *Proceso* in a September 13, 1993, interview that the "northerner's" movement was taken over by the Emiliano Zapata Peasant Organization (OCEZ) and the National Independent Emiliano Zapata Peasant Alliance (ANCIEZ) and that these organizations then split into two factions, one calling for an armed uprising and one calling for more moderate tactics.

> We do not know at what exact moment the OCEZ and the ANCIEZ, which are extremist organizations, came in and took over the northerner's movement. We learned that the northern advisers were gradually leaving. It seems that the OCEZ and the ANCIEZ are the same thing, with different names and fronts.
>
> They are developing as ejido unions, or production centers, depending on the needs of the region. And on top of this comes all the idealization of the political struggle, which is particularly violent, and the preparation for it.
>
> They have a network of economic and organizational advisers. That is how they keep people in line. And behind that mask, they have also organized the whole radio situation, which is how the entire jungle stays in touch.[50]

Marcos and his idealist compatriots were made responsible for military organizing and training, following precepts that Marcos attributed to

> Pancho Villa, as far as regular army tactics are concerned, and Emiliano Zapata, with respect to the interchange between guerilla and peasant. We got the rest out of a manual of the Mexican army that fell into our hands, and a small manual from the Pentagon, and some work by a French general whose name I can't remember.[51]

Gradually, the movement acquired weapons, from several sources, according to Marcos:

> [We got weapons from] three sources. [sic] A small portion comes from the "work of ants," of buying arms here and there. Another important source is the Mexican police and army involved in the anti-drug battle. When they arrest drug traffickers, they seize their weapons, but they only turn over only a small portion of the weapons to their superiors, the rest are sold in the black market. That's how we bought AK-47, M-16, and other arms. They thought they were selling to other drug traffickers and that they would soon enough arrest them and resell the weapons. The third source was the *guardias blancas* [hired gunmen] of the ranchers, trained by the security forces and the army. They had good weapons and last year began to receive Uzis. Finally, there are the weapons of the peasants themselves, shotguns and rudimentary things. We don't have as many weapons as we would like, nor ammunition.[52]

Over time, the movement began to recruit from among the broader peasantry.

> As far as the peasants are concerned, the EZLN arose as a self-defense group to defend against the ranchers' hired gunmen, who try to take their land and maltreat them, limiting the social and political advancement of the Indians. So they took up arms so as not to be defenseless. Then, later, the comrades saw it wasn't enough to do self-defense of a single ejido or community but rather to establish alliances with others and to begin to make up military and paramilitary contingents on a larger scale, still for the purpose of self-defense.[53]

Before long, youngsters from surrounding regions were coming to the EZLN for training. When young men of the region reached the age of Mexican compulsory military service, many families would urge them to gain training in the mountains rather than with the army—especially after the Salinas government began to pursue what Marcos sarcastically describes as the "brilliant idea" of reforming Article 27 of the Constitution and the Agrarian Code. "That was an important catalyst. The reforms negated any legal possibility of obtaining land, and it was land that was at the basis of peasants' self-defense."[54] Furthermore, by changing the law, the government removed a crucial reason for peasants to try to work within the law.

Salinas de Gortari's reform of Article 27 of the Mexican Constitution and of the Agrarian Code—the very legislation that made land reform a central tenet of the Mexican state—was in fact just one more step in his government's project to restructure the Mexican economy by removing government involvement and support of sectors thought to be "antimodern." Some of the restructuring had been forced on Mexico during the Miguel de la Madrid presidency (1982–88), as part of an austerity program required by the international banking community for bailing Mexico out from its debt crisis. The austerity program dried up subsidies to peasants for fertilizer and other chemical inputs and eroded price supports for crops. But de la Madrid's restructuring had stemmed from a paucity of economic resources; Salinas de Gortari's reflected a change of will.

Salinas's advisors reached a consensus that Mexico's existing peasantry had to be subjected to major surgery, transformed and absorbed into the modernization of agriculture to increase the productivity of millions of peasant-held hectares used for crops not competitive on world markets, or worked by labor that could be put to more productive use elsewhere. Market subsidies for peasant crops, such as the transport subsidies that the Mexican Coffee Institute had negotiated with the Union of Unions in eastern Chiapas, had to be eliminated. The entire system of agrarian credits needed to be overhauled, advisors concluded, to circumvent corrupt practices wherein bankers and peasants were colluding in fraudulent claims of crop failure to renege on loans. Furthermore, land reform itself should be brought to a standstill to prevent further land from being absorbed into inefficient peasant production. Thus, the advisors advocated the privatization and commercialization of peasant and Indian-held parcels.

Salinas forced these changes through the Mexican congress in 1992. They were denounced by critics as the death knell for the peasantry, and as potentially devastating to agrarian communities as the Liberal Reform laws of 1856 and 1863 that had robbed Indian communities of their lands and plunged them into penury. The "reform" of Article 27 is certain to have galvanized peasant antagonism to the national state, and may well have contributed to the EZLN decision, in January 1993, that EZLN forces were sufficiently organized and trained, and its alliances with sympathizers and potential supporters developed enough, to launch a revolution. According to Marcos, it was at the end of January 1993 "that the Clandestine Committee decided 'We're going to take up arms,' and they ordered me, 'You take charge of it, we'll give you so much time, and you set the date within those limits.'"[55]

At that moment, evidently, the EZLN was not particularly concerned with NAFTA, the North American Free Trade Agreement passed by the Mexican, Canadian, and United States governments in 1993 and inaugurated on January 1, 1994, the date finally chosen for the EZLN uprising. Although EZLN proclamations first identified NAFTA as having inspired their revolution, it is apparent that the designation of NAFTA was a pretext. As Marcos explained to reporters who asked why NAFTA's inaugural date had been selected for the uprising,

> It's like the myth of the facemasks. We used facemasks because of the cold. But suddenly the facemasks caught on with the people, and so now we keep them on. We had not planned to rise up on January 1 . . . .
>
> We thought about various dates, taking various factors into account. For example, we needed to show clearly that we weren't drug traffickers. We had to do something related to cities, the pretext couldn't be just about rural conditions so that they couldn't write us off in the jungle, as they did in the incident in the mountains of Corralchén, that garrison of ours they discovered, when they decided we were [a fringe group], marijuana growers, or Guatemalans. We didn't say anything, because we were watching to see what would happen.[56]

In May 1993, the army had raided an EZLN garrison in the remote colony of Corralchén. Although first reports described the raid as having routed out a guerrilla camp, complete with underground bunkers and a scale model of the municipal headtown of Ocosingo, the government subsequently downplayed the reports. At the time, acknowledging the existence of a guerrilla movement in Chiapas would have endangered the chances that the US Congress would accept NAFTA, as it finally did after a battle hard fought and won by U.S. President Bill Clinton in the summer of 1993.

Marcos continued:

Then there was the problem of the civilian population, and our concern as to what would happen to the guerrilla cause if we attacked the civilian population. For a *guerrillero,* who will die for his cause, nothing is more repugnant than to harm civilians. It's worse than being captured by the army.

Then there were logistical questions, apart from political ones. For example, when would our food reserves be greatest, given that the war would be long, that we would be surrounded, that they would drive us into the mountains, so [the uprising] had to begin just after harvest, when we could get money together.

The truth of the matter is that the decision about when to rise up didn't take national politics into account. That's not so important to the comrades, not so much as not being able to stomach things any longer, regardless of national or international conditions.[57]

IV. OIL AND THE CRISIS IN MEXICAN AGRICULTURE

When I think about the impact of energy development on Mexico's southeast, I ponder the situation of two young men whose divergent experiences reflect the contradictions of change that development has brought. One is the gaunt youth from a frontier colony east of Las Margaritas who, shivering, hitched a ride with me in 1991 on his way to Villahermosa, Tabasco to look for work—any work—in construction near the oil fields. The other is a young man who invested earnings from such work into a combination of farming and a small business selling flowers and vegetables at a market stand in Ocozocuautla, fifty miles away from his home and children in Zinacantán, who was able to purchase a pickup truck to haul wholesale produce to market.

Both young men came from rural areas whose agrarian production was thrown into crisis by energy development in the 1970s, which devalued traditional crops and drew peasants into dependence on jobs far from home to help support their families. Mexico's 1982 debt crisis forced peasants back into farming, which they had to intensify or diversify into crops such as coffee that require purchased chemical inputs and entail risky credits and markets. Some people, like the young man from Zinacantán who lives close to roads and developed markets, have made good by combining farming with nonfarming enterprise. Others, such as those from Las Margaritas frontier areas who invested heavily in coffee production, have been devastated by the collapse of world coffee prices and the government's withdrawal of credits and production subsidies. These young men's experiences illustrate the uneven pace of development in rural Mexico and the extent to which participation in the global economy brought new opportunities even as it undermined the agricultural basis of peasant life and created an unprecedented gap between rich and poor in peasant communities.

Their stories also reflect a new reality of peasant life, which is no longer strictly defined by food production. The vast majority of peasant households now participate in some kind of wage work or commercial enterprise in addition to farming. Peasants in today's Mexico double as masons, carpenters, ditch diggers, truck drivers, small store owners, and tailors, and their vocations echo changes in many rural areas of the developing world. The changes stretch the concept of "peasantry" to new limits by encompassing people—including the Zapatista women who want the chance to become truck drivers—who still

> have some ability to produce their own food, or have a close kinship connection to people who have some ability to produce their own food, or interact in a local economy with people who have some ability to produce their own food . . . . This category includes . . . *petty commodity producers* . . . who produce things for sale or live by trading in local markets . . . ; and *semiproletarians* . . . who currently work for wages but who also depend on food production or petty commodity production by themselves or their kinsmen for survival.[1]

That indigenous peasants should participate in a variety of non-farming activities is not in itself new. Colonial Chiapas depended on indigenous labor for more than food production. In the nineteenth century, indigenous peoples were forced from their villages and pressed into service for nominal wages on the coastal coffee plantations and lowland ranches. Indians literally built San Cristóbal at the turn of the century.[2] What has changed for peasants—as a consequence of Mexico's energy development—is the dramatic growth of nonagricultural work and the increasing integration of peasant economies into national and international markets.

We must understand these changes if we are to appreciate why some of the Zapatistas want to be truck drivers, are demanding work as well as land, consumer goods such as refrigerators and televisions as well as housing, and schooling for real skills as well as basics such as health care.

The world of the Zapatistas, furthermore, is *not just* that of eastern Chiapas. Like others throughout rural Chiapas, the Zapatistas circulate in an economy in which wage work, coffee production, cattle, and commerce mix and move people, stretching the meaning and boundaries of community over a wide landscape.

Crisis in Agriculture

Energy development changed the face of Mexico's southeastern region during the 1960s and 1970s. From 1936 onward, when Mexico nationalized the oil fields held by foreign firms, the country developed petroleum for Mexico's internal needs. But after the Organization of Petroleum Exporting Countries (OPEC) shocked the world economy by raising oil prices in 1972, Mexico decided to export petroleum and began to expand coastal and inland oil production. After oil exploration uncovered vast reserves along the Tabasco coast of the Gulf of Mexico, the government found it easy to secure loans from a world banking system glutted by petrodollars. It used the borrowed money to expand oil production and to underwrite ambitious new projects of development. In Chiapas, the government completed two major hydroelectric power projects that had been started in the 1960s on the Grijalva River between the Guatemalan border and the Gulf of Mexico. As energy development shifted into high gear, the southeastern region began to supply Mexico with half its hydroelectric power and much of its oil for export.[3]

During this oil-led boom, Mexican agriculture declined as the country experienced symptoms of what development economists refer to as the oil syndrome, or Dutch disease. This concept refers to how export booms undermine other sectors of a country's economy, a phenomenon that economists nicknamed Dutch disease in their analyses of the negative impact of North Sea gas development on Dutch manufacturing. As oil exports boomed in Holland and other petroleum producing nations, each country suffered unexpected setbacks in other sectors such as manufacturing, agriculture, or production of other tradeables (exports). Economists explained that the export boom tended to overvalue the exporting country's currency and caused labor and other resources to shift into oil production or sectors producing non-tradeables such as construction and infrastructure. In Mexico's case, while industry expanded from 27 percent of the gross domestic product (GDP) in 1965 to 38 percent in 1982, the contribution of agriculture to GDP fell by half, from 14 percent to just 7 percent.[4]

Figure 4.1 **Trends in Mexican Energy Development.** As world oil prices rose after the OPEC crisis (A), Mexico began to develop oil fields for exports which grew during the 1980s. Meanwhile, government expenditures had risen sharply in anticipation of oil revenues. Mexico borrowed heavily to fund expenditures (B), and external debt swelled, generating the debt crisis when world oil prices turned downward in 1982. During the period of energy development up to 1982, Mexican agriculture declined by half (C) from 14% to 7% of the gross domestic product (GDP), while industry grew. Mexican agriculture recovered slightly after the 1982 debt crisis.

Peasants left the countryside in droves. Many migrated to Mexico City, other cities, or to the United States to look for work. Despite the agrarian redistribution that took place during Luis Echeverría's 1970–1976 presidency, agricultural production shifted away from basic staples such as corn to fruits, vegetables, and meat

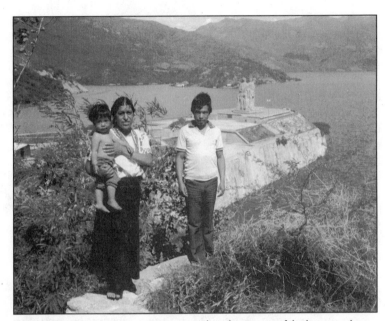

Photo 4.1 **The Chicoasen Dam.** A Zinacanteco couple at Chicoasen, one of the three major dams built on the Grijalva River.

destined for middle class consumption and export. Mexico devoted more foreign exchange to purchasing corn from the United States to feed the poorest 40 percent of the population, whose share of the national wealth had not grown since the 1950s. Mexicans quickly came to believe their agriculture was in crisis, even as other sectors of their economy boomed. By 1980, Mexico was importing 25 percent of its corn. Mexican politicians, chastened by American talk of using grain exports as a tool in foreign policy, began to fear that corn imports could jeopardize Mexico's sovereignty.[5]

This food crisis exacerbated Mexican scholars' debates about the place of peasants in Mexican society, and whether they hindered or aided agrarian development. Some argued that peasant production was inefficient and did not contribute to Mexico's growing comparative advantage in producing export commodities such as tomatoes, or beef and animal feed crops. Pro-peasant analysts argued that production of maize was indispensable and that declines in maize production could be reversed by allowing peasants fair access to inputs, credits, and markets, to counterbalance inroads that agribusiness was making in the rural economy.[6] The 1976–82 López Portillo administration heeded these arguments. It established mechanisms for credits such as those granted to the Union of Unions in eastern Chiapas in 1980, and launched the Mexican Food System (SAM) to improve the distribution of food to the poor and reinvigorate peasant production through federal subsidies for fertilizer and for other inputs, credits, and price supports. The government also reoriented road-building programs to increase the number of feeder roads linking isolated settlements to national markets.

Mexico's development boom came to an abrupt halt in 1982 when world oil prices declined sharply and Mexico found itself unable to service the huge external debt that the country had taken on during the boom (see Figure 4.1)[7]. The government curtailed subsidies for peasant production, reawakening the debate over policy towards peasants.[8] After 1988, Salinas de Gortari pushed ahead with restructuring the economy through policies leading to NAFTA and to the decision to dismantle the agrarian reform by rewriting Article 27 of the Constitution and the Agrarian Code—one of the actions precipitating the Zapatista rebellion.

Energy Development in Chiapas

I learned about the impact of energy development on hamlets tucked into the mountainsides of central Chiapas in a 1981 economic survey I conducted in Apas, Zinacantán.[9] Fourteen years before, in 1967, virtually every Apas household had almost exclusively farmed milpa. In 1981, I learned that men in household after household had gone off to work on government construction projects near the oil fields or at dams being built for the federal electrical commission. Zinacantecos told me that they could earn far more money in such work than they could by farming corn, and most families farmed only a patch of their land.

Manuel was about fifteen years old when he first went off to a construction job:

Others from Apas were going off to work far away to earn money. They worked at Concordia. There used to be a place called Old Concordia, but when the dam was built at Angostura, it flooded Old Concordia, and so they built a completely new Concordia. And that was the first place I went to look for work, along with others from Apas who were going there, like Antonio, who's now my brother-in-law.

I asked him to take me along, but at the time I didn't speak Spanish and I was afraid of ladinos. "Who knows if you'll get taken on, get given work right away?" Antonio asked me. "Let me go find out." So we went off to work at New Concordia, where the work boss, a contractor, hired me to fill in the ditch for a pipeline for drinking water. I worked for two weeks, but I barely endured it because I didn't understand Spanish and was afraid of the ladinos.

Most Zinacantecos, together with indigenous people from throughout Chiapas who flocked to construction jobs in the 1970s, lacked Spanish language and work skills and had to begin work as unskilled ditch diggers or porters. Many of them picked up Spanish and learned vocational skills on the job. After trying out work at New Concordia, Manuel took up a job assisting a ladino mason, who taught him the trade and helped him improve his Spanish.

"Can you read and write?" he asked me. "Yes, a little bit." "Well, why don't you write down the names of the tools that we use," he suggested. "Write it down, I'll tell you all the names," and he showed me each of the tools and told me what each was called. So I wrote down the name of each tool and what it was used for, and I wrote down the Tzotzil names as well as the Spanish words. And that way, gradually I learned Spanish. So later, when I went to other work, I was no longer scared to go. I had become accustomed to the work and I understood Spanish.

Manuel accompanied this mason from one construction site to another, working near each of the dams that the government built along the Grijalva at Angostura, Chicoasen, and Malpaso. Often working overtime, he earned very good money and used it to marry and to build a tile-roofed house back in Apas, a rarity there at a time when most homes were still made of mud brick and thatch. He paid others to do the building and watch over his milpa while he was away.

Figure 4.2 **Sites of Energy Development.**

Figure 4.3 **Declines in Agriculture, 1960 to 1980.** Agriculture dominated Chiapas in 1960, claiming over 85% of the economically active population in most rural townships. By 1980, that figure had declined to less than 75% in most areas, reflecting national trends during the 1970s.

Figure 4.4 **Growth in Construction and Transport, 1960 to 1980.** As agriculture declined during the 1970s, construction and transport increased in areas near oil and hydroelectric development.

Construction work began to differentiate Zinacantecos as some of them acquired enough skills, tools, and capital to become independent masons or carpenters. They could then function as private contractors, hiring other indigenous people to work for them. Juan, another Zinacanteco, told me about how he launched himself as an independent contractor in work near Villahermosa, Tabasco:

Photo 4.2 **Construction Skills**. This Zinacanteco uses the skills he learned during the development boom to build a house for a well-to-do neighbor who is a trucker.

I'd learned how to do almost everything. I'd seen how the work was done, building with stone, with brick, with cement block, tile, mosaic, plastering, and so forth. I had bought some tools, a trowel, hammer, plumb line, level, T square, chisel, pick, shovel, and wheel barrow. So I decided to seek a piecework contract. There was a contractor I worked with who saw what I could do, and I asked him if he wouldn't subcontract me work by the meter. And he agreed, turning the blueprints over to me to work from. I didn't really know how to read the blueprint very well, but I could more or less tell where the walls were supposed to go, where cement posts were supposed to be, and I did the job. I had a friend, Mariano, and I hired him to lay bricks for me.

At first I did piecework this way; later I began to contract directly. At the time, a mason's weekly wage was 80,000 pesos, but I found I could take contracts from the engineer paying 4000 pesos per meter of construction. Mariano and I could complete 80 meters per week. I would get 320,000 pesos for the job and pay Mariano 100,000 per week out of that, more than he could earn as a mason, and twice what he would have earned as a mason's assistant. We worked hard, and I earned a lot of money, and then I quit.

Juan used his earnings to purchase a market stall in Jaltenango where he took up wholesale-retail produce trade as an independent business. Many Zinacantecos started up small market businesses at this time. Others invested in trucks and took up work in transport.[10]

By the height of the boom in 1981, off-farm activities had differentiated the wealthy from the poor and diversified the livelihoods of almost all Zinacantecos. Men of the wealthiest households in Apas were heavily into small businesses. Some were in commerce as wholesale-retail traders in produce; others purchased trucks and started transport businesses. Poorer men were almost all engaged in wage work. Among the workers, young and middle-aged men worked predominantly as unskilled hired hands on construction. Older men combined work as hired field hands with small-scale farming on their own. Overall, Zinacantecos had all but abandoned the farming of maize. As will be discussed in the next chapter, these changes also made women, most of whom stayed behind in the hamlet, more dependent on cash incomes than they had been when men and women worked together in household production and consumption.[11]

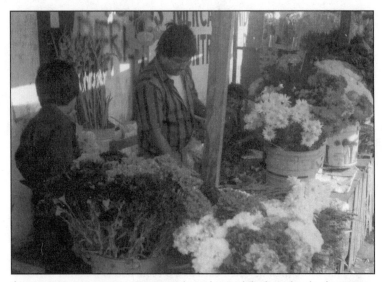

Photo 4.3 **Peasant Commerce.** Peasant men have taken up wholesale-retail produce businesses to supplement farming. Many Zinacantecos specialize in selling flowers at stands they lease or own in markets throughout central Chiapas.

Photo 4.4 **Indigenous Truckers.** A Zinacanteco seeks advice about his overheated radiator from a fellow trucker.

Peasants from other municipios also reconfigured their livelihoods in response to opportunities that beckoned from the zones of rapidly expanding Gulf Coast oil production and rapid metropolitan growth in Tabasco and Chiapas.[12] The 1980 census figures show that indigenous people from the rural areas of Chiapas resettled into the Gulf Coast oil zone and into metropolitan centers of Villahermosa, Tuxtla Gutiérrez, San Cristóbal de las Casas, and Tapachula. Colonists also flowed into the frontier areas of eastern Chiapas. Throughout the region, the proportion of the working population active in agriculture declined dramatically as people shifted into nonagricultural employment in commerce, transport and construction (see Figures 4.3 and 4.4).

It is important to emphasize that these effects of the "oil syndrome" did not affect all areas of agriculture in exactly the same way. While maize farming declined throughout the countryside, some kinds of agrarian production resisted or even advanced against the tide of agrarian decline. Close to the oil fields in Tabasco, where peasants could combine wage work with small-scale farming, lucrative peasant cultivation of cacao flourished. Larger-scale private cacao producers did not fare as well as the peasants, whose smaller scale of production allowed their families to integrate wage work and cultivation. Another factor favoring these peasant cacao producers was a cooperative marketing organization, similar to that developed by the Union of Unions (UU) for coffee in eastern Chiapas, that allowed small-scale cacao producers to circumvent middle-men and get better prices for their products.[13]

Restructuring Peasant Agriculture

As the 1982 debt crisis unfolded, the government cut employment in the public sector, curtailed development projects, and laid off thousands of construction workers. Zinacantecos remember their foremen telling them that "the President wants you to go back to farming."[14]

Many Zinacantecos did indeed return to farming, but did not give up off-farm vocations. They were in a fortunate position vis-à-vis other indigenous communities because most Zinacantecos lived near or along the Pan American highway and had easy access to the off-farm urban work that, although it became scarcer and scarcer, didn't dry up entirely. Many Zinacantecos revived their milpas as part of a "diversified portfolio" of livelihoods.[15] Wealthier wholesale-retail produce vendors and truckers scheduled work for their businesses and maize farming in a rotating fashion, using family labor or hired helpers to meet overlapping work responsibilities. Poorer Zinacantecos sought seasonal construction jobs during months when maize fields were less demanding of their time, and many of them worked as field hands for other Zinacantecos.

Figure 4.5 **Changing Intensity of Apas Farmland Use.** The proportion of farmland in use (shaded parcels) slackened notably from 1964 (A) to 1973 (B) as Zinacantecos shifted to off-farm activities. After 1982, as opportunities for off-farm work decreased, Zinacantecos reinvigorated highland farming by using chemical inputs to farm plots with less fallowing. By 1988 (C), the more intense use of Apas farmland had eliminated most fallow land.

Zinacantecos began to transform their farming by using fertilizer and herbicides to intensify their cultivation in the highlands. By using fertilizers, they could farm plots year after year without fallowing. Doing so effectively increased the number of acres Zinacantecos had at their disposal in their *ejidos*, reducing the amount of land they needed to rent in the lowlands and saving them the costs of transport to and from lowland fields. The herbicides substantially reduced the work of weeding the milpa, reducing or eliminating the need to hire workers to help, and freeing up family labor to do things in the off-farm economy.

These changes contributed to the gap that had begun to distinguish well-off from poor Zinacantecos during the development boom. Those who had established themselves as independent contractors, truckers, or successful wholesale-retail market vendors had money in their pockets from such off-farm work to pay for the chemical inputs being used in farming. Often they farmed at the expense of poor Zinacantecos who didn't have financial resources to pay for fertilizer and weed sprays, even if they held land to farm. Many poorer Zinacantecos began to rent their *ejido* plots to their wealthier neighbors who could afford the chemical inputs. One wealthy trader, for example, recently rented the fields of twenty-five other Zinacantecos who could not afford chemical inputs. He hired the parcels' owners as laborers to farm corn for him, "putting his money to work" at others' expense. Such arrangements are to be found in *ejidos* throughout Mexico.

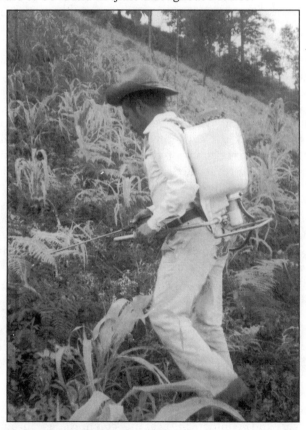

Photo 4.5 **Herbicide Use.** Herbicides and fertilizer have become widely used in farming corn, reducing the labor needed to clear weeds. Because both are expensive, not all peasants can afford to farm.

Some Zinacantecos formed cooperative associations—small business collectives—for trucking and flower vending, similar to those established by many Mexican peasant groups for the production and distribution of cash crops such as organic coffee. The associations helped members combine on-and-off farm production, and gained access to credit from banks or the government, which often gave them political support as well. These associations often claim to be peasant organizations, even though some of their members do not farm land for subsistence. The Zinacanteco truckers, for example, said they unionized in order to obtain routes to transport the produce grown in their communities. In fact, the richest truckers transport flowers that Zinacanteco wholesalers purchase in Mexico City for resale throughout Chiapas.[16]

Indians in other highland communities, Chamula for example, experienced greater adversity when wage work employment slowed after 1982, especially if they had little or no land of their own to farm. Chamulas are among the most land-poor of the highland Indians in Chiapas. After 1982, most Chamulas found they could not go back to the work they had once done as hired field hands in the central depression of the Grijalva basin. Landowners, like peasants, had reallocated their production during the energy-led boom. Much of the land once rented to peasants—in effect for sharecropping—had been converted to grasslands for cattle. Furthermore, milpa-farming peasants like the Zinacantecos, for whom Chamulas had also labored, used much less labor because of their access to chemical inputs. Many Chamulas found their families pushed into desperate straits after 1982.[17]

While many indigenous people were set back by unemployment after 1982, a minority did profit from trucking and other commercial enterprises they had taken up during the boom. The development of peasant trucking has been a double-edged sword, on the one hand allowing peasants to retain shipping profits that once flowed out of the countryside into Ladino truckers' pockets, and on the other hand enabling peasant truckers to profit at the expense of their rural compatriots. As in the case of Zinacantán, the accumulation of transport capital has emerged as a major axis of power and conflict in peasant communities throughout Chiapas. In Tenejapa, trucker organizations act as a major local political force,[18] just as they do in Zinacantán.

The hardships of unemployed and impoverished Chamulas and other poor peasants are comparable to the circumstances that led Rolando, a Major in the EZLN, to join the rebel army around 1986. At the height of the oil boom, Rolando told San Francisco Chronicle reporter Robert Collier, he migrated to Tuxtla Gutiérrez, where he lived with Tzeltal relatives and attended school through second grade. Then he took up construction work in Tuxtla. After the 1982 crisis, he could only get construction work at starvation wages. "You go to look for a decent job and they ask you for a resume . . . , [a]nd of course, I have no resume," he told Collier. He returned to his jungle hometown, but conditions were untenable there as well. He joined one of the independent organizations to press the government for assistance.

> So we went on a march, asking the government for land, and they beat us back with clubs. We kept organizing, but you have to pay to send delegations to San Cristóbal and Tuxtla and Mexico City. It was just going around in circles, and we didn't have any money.

Rolando joined the EZLN out of frustration. "What future do I, or any of us here, have in the new Mexico? I can sell or export my own cheap labor. But I have nothing else."[19]

Not everyone in the Selva Lacandona or other areas of eastern Chiapas suffered because of the boom and bust. Colonization burgeoned at the time, and many settled down, farming milpa, coffee, and pasturing livestock. Settlers who arrived first were best off because they were the earliest to secure land. Later arrivals usually had to work for established settlers before gaining land and enough security to farm independently. As Guatemalan refugees flowed into some regions, they took up work at the bottom tier of the wage scale. Gaps between land-rich and land-poor grew when credits became available through the Union of Unions after 1980, in conjunction with federal support for peasant agriculture through the SAM, and as more settlers invested in coffee production.

Nuevo Huistán—the Cañadas region colony in Las Margaritas described in Chapter Two—experienced an increase in tension between rich and poor by 1983. As mentioned before, Nuevo Huistán derived seven-eighths of its income from cash crops and its three hundred head of cattle, horses, and mules.[20] A roadway had established the town as a node of transport and trade, linking

more isolated areas of the Cañadas region of Las Margaritas outward to regional and national markets. Commerce distinguished
settlers into a wealthier group, involved in bulking and marketing
cash crops, and poorer settlers, who relied upon wage work. By
1983, when anthropologist Juan Pohlenz surveyed Nuevo Huistán,
this small colony of 316 people had as many truck owning families
as the Zinacanteco hamlet of Apas, which I studied in the central
highlands of Chiapas, even though Nuevo Huistán is a smaller
community, about one-third the size of Apas.[21]

Austerity hit eastern Chiapas hard after 1982. The region's
mixed economy of timber, corn, coffee, and cattle suffered under
the eventual removal of fertilizer subsidies. Salinas, after taking
office in 1988, dismantled INMECAFE, which had guaranteed
markets for the Union of Union's coffee. The world price of coffee
fell by 50 percent in 1989, leaving coffee producers in the lurch as
their incomes plummeted and their debts spiraled out of control.[22]
Throughout Chiapas—not just in the east—the hard won gains of
peasants who had taken out loans to finance coffee production
evaporated as banks foreclosed on loans and took over land, cattle,
or other collateral. The crisis contributed to defection into the
Zapatista camp from the Union of Unions and the ARIC-Union of
Unions, both of which had promoted peasant coffee production as
a way of gaining government credits and assistance in marketing.

Energy development, with its boom in the 1970s and bust after
1982, whiplashed the agrarian economy of southeastern Mexico,
leaving both profit and devastation in its wake and sharpening the
differentials of wealth and power to which the Zapatista rebellion
responds.

V. THE TOLL OF RESTRUCTURING ON LIVES AND COMMUNITIES

During the oil boom of the 1970s, a new player began to take center stage in the indigenous hamlets of Chiapas. Money. As wage work became more readily available, cash-based transactions between people, even among kin, began to replace exchanges of services and obligations, and purchased foods and commodities began to replace those grown or made at home. This switch brought tremendous change to life in the countryside, transforming the traditional economy, accelerating changes in social and political relationships and, in some ways, altering the traditional roles of men and women. The new reliance on cash gave distinct advantage to some members of peasant society, particularly young men and those with small businesses, many of whom have begun to make the kinds of changes in rural production envisioned by government plans of restructuring. But it has added new burdens to the lives of others, especially women and those men with less education and property.

In the previous chapter, we looked at the large-scale impact oil and hydroelectric development had on Mexico and Chiapas: how the macroeconomic shifts, the policy revisions and the undertaking of massive public projects drew peasants from their villages and into a new type of give-and-take with the regional economy that has restructured peasant agriculture. In this chapter, we go back to the village to see how these changes have been played out *within* communities.

We will examine changes of the sort taking place around the world as peasants and workers are drawn increasingly into global markets that displace subsistence economies and erode the ability of many to weather downturns in economic cycles.[1]

We will focus on two Maya towns in the central highlands of Chiapas: the hamlet of Apas in the municipio of Zinacantán, as well as hamlets in the neighboring municipio of Chamula, the most populous and one of the poorest of the Indian townships. These neighboring towns refract the shared experience of energy development much like two crystals placed slightly differently in the same light. Although the circumstances described are specific, they typify many of the pressures experienced by peasant communities throughout Chiapas. Both Zinacantán and Chamula have been much studied by anthropologists, but Chamula has come to symbolize the "typical" Indian town in the minds of many ladinos and nonindigenous Mexicans.[2]

Perhaps the most pronounced difference between the two municipios today is their access to land. Although Zinacantecos are by no means land rich, a majority of Zinacanteco families still maintain small plots of land that they can use to supplement their incomes from other sources or use to provide at least a bare minimum of food for their households. The majority of Chamula families, on the other hand, either have no land or are unable to eke out even the most meager subsistence from their tiny plots and so must either hire themselves out as field hands to others, including Zinacantecos, or leave their communities to seek wage work elsewhere. While the safety net that land provides to Zinacantecos is diminishing rapidly, Chamulas have already lost that net and are living at the very margins of existence. Their financial straits are further exacerbated by the fact that many Chamula hamlets are not linked to major roads, which makes it expensive and difficult to transport produce or handicrafts to market in San Cristóbal de las Casas or other metropolitan centers.

At the heart of both communities lies the question of the changing nature of maize cultivation. As agriculture changed in rural Mexico, so did the nature of peasant society. It may seem contradictory to place such emphasis on agriculture after pointing out in the previous chapter that most peasants no longer focus exclusively on food production, but the shifting fortunes of Mexican agriculture have created real differences in the way people live. And even the wealthiest peasants who make their living primarily in such nonagricultural enterprises such as trucking and retailing identify themselves as farmers. Emotional ties to the land persist even where the practical ties to the land have withered. Peasants still consider the land their basis for survival.

After the 1982 economic crisis, when further dam building was put off and construction abated, Zinacantecos returned on a smaller scale to farming maize while continuing, as much as possible, in the pursuits they had begun during the boom years, such as selling food in market stalls or working for wages in San Cristóbal de las Casas. But as we noted in the previous chapter, corn cultivation had been transformed due to the increased use of chemical fertilizers and weed killers, funded by government subsidies and also peasants' off-farm earnings. In the years between the boom and bust, the land became accustomed to chemical inputs and fields were not nearly as productive without them. Simple tools and equipment (machete, hoe, billhook, bags) and a reserve of corn sufficient to feed one's household and field workers were no longer enough to enable a Zinacanteco household to farm. Fertilizer and weed sprays had to be purchased. Workers, if they were hired, no longer waited for payment in kind after the harvest; they expected payment in cash at the time of their work. Local truckers had to be paid to haul the harvest home.

The chemically intensive, but not labor intensive, method of farming also undermined the social organization of many peasant hamlets by removing a certain safety net of mutual dependence that kept young and poor people who needed food bound to their older and wealthier neighbors who, when weeding and cultivating had been done by hand, needed people to help them. Prior to the 1980s, Zinacantán had been a place where the disadvantaged could count on others for their basic livelihoods as long as they were willing to help out with corn production. But as maize cultivation was displaced from its once central place in Zinacanteco life, the poor found themselves utterly marginalized; their labor in the fields was no longer required and they lacked any way of earning the money necessary to buy food.

In Chamula, the fallout of the 1982 debt crisis was even more severe. Anthropologist Diane Rus, who lived in the Chamula hamlet of K'at'ixtik for many years, found that most families were able to extract only a tiny portion (5 percent in 1977) of their food needs from their corn fields before the oil boom. After the bust, that portion diminished even further. Men who had been accustomed to wage work on coffee plantations to make up the shortfall in subsistence suddenly found themselves unable to find jobs.

Consequently, many men were forced into the unstable temporary work force and began to leave K'at'ixtik for long periods of time looking for work, leaving women to single-handedly hold their homes and families together.[3]

Land and the Changing Economy

Owning and farming one's own land is a relatively recent phenomenon in Zinacantán. Prior to the 1940s, only a handful of wealthy families held tracts of land; other Zinacantecos worked for them. In 1940, almost all married men in Apas received *ejidal* land, substantially ameliorating differences among them based on property. For the first time, every household in Apas farmed milpa.

At first Zinacantecos concentrated on farming in the highlands using labor-intensive swidden, or slash-and-burn, cultivation. But the *ejido* could not sustain the Zinacanatecos' population, and the number of landless families increased once again. Zinacantecos then began to rent marginal farmlands in the Grijalva River valley from ranchers who were eager to convert scrub forest to grazing land. As roadways opened up the Grijalva valley during the 1960s, Zinacantecos followed them. They rented little-used marginal ranch land, reaped the higher yields obtainable from fallow lands, and moved on. Farming was still quite labor intensive and every household member played a role in growing and harvesting the crops. Some Zinacantecos employed workers from Chamula. They farmed for profit as well as subsistence and sold much of their crop directly to the federal corn warehouse system established in the early 1960s. Some began to experiment with hybrid seed and chemical weed sprays.[4]

Not all Zinacantecos were able to reap benefits from the land. The labor intensive farming methods gave the greatest advantage to older Zinacantecos who were able to maintain an adequate supply of labor either by using their children as workers or by amassing large numbers of followers who would work in their fields in exchange for political favors. During the 1950s and 1960s, a system of costly and time-consuming courtships developed that left young couples financially obligated to continue working in their parents' fields rather than farming independently.

By the 1970s, the population density of the highlands of Chiapas had almost negated the benefits of land reform. As noted in the previous chapter, Zinacantecos and other indigenous peoples found it increasingly difficult to find land to rent in the lowlands, where ranchers had turned over huge sections of property to cattle raising. Some peasants who continued to rent lowland plots lost money if they were unable to wait until after harvest time to sell their crops—the prices prevailing at harvest were the lowest of the year; wealthier Zinacantecos with cash to spare from other enterprises could wait to sell their crops until later in the season. Because the return on the average plot of land was so low, and because the chemical inputs were so expensive, many poorer Zinacantecos—even those with land of their own—no longer had the means to farm unless they borrowed money. By 1981, Zinacantecos had virtually abandoned lowland rental agriculture. The Chamula men from K'at'ixtik who rent lowland plots find their money completely eaten up by the costs of farming—fertilizers, herbicides, labor and transportation. The situation, according to Rus, is so dismal that "it is commonly remarked that men are more likely to lose money than make it on lowland farming."[5]

One thing that stymies economic planners and development officials is the fact that even though farming is only marginally more profitable in the highlands, today most families attempt to raise milpa on their communal plots if at all possible. The returns are lower to family labor than prevailing wages and rarely high enough to justify hiring field hands. However, this seemingly unprofitable undertaking can sometimes be offset by the other enterprises that invariably make up a family's income. It is also true that the regional economy probably cannot offer every individual full employment and so "working for food" provides a basis for subsistence. Some Zinacantecos have no land at all and so must either seek food or make money to buy it in other ways. Years ago, there would have been little need to distinguish between "seeking food" and "making money" because most peasants were assured of at least being fed if they worked for other villagers in corn production. But now that those "jobs" are not available, a cash-based economic system has emerged and has led to further hardships for the poorer sector of peasant society.

In the years preceding the oil boom, when families were too poor to feed themselves, their members could seek food by working as field hands. Employers were expected to provide food and lodging for their workers, and instead of paying cash, they paid wages in corn at harvest time. Most Zinacanteco employers today do not board their field hands but simply pay cash wages, as do most nonindigenous employers. The wages are often not enough to guarantee a minimum subsistence.

Many women, by contrast, still work for food. Women from households with shortfalls in food—typically women from poor households, or women without husbands or children old enough to help with farming—may take up piecework for other women. They may make tortillas and hardtack, using the other woman's corn, but supplying their own firewood, and accepting as pay an amount of corn equal to that which they process.

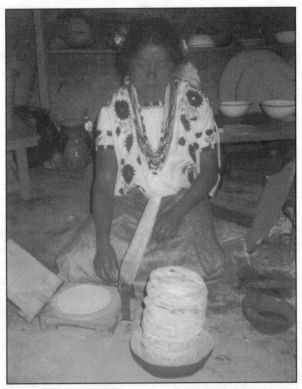

Photo 5.1 **Making Tortillas.** A woman prepares tortillas for a ritual gathering. Herbicides have reduced the labor needed in the fields as well as the cooking needed to feed field hands.

Some Zinacanteco women, predominantly those who are elderly, poor, or widowed, also work as remunerated field hands, especially in milpas close to home in the highlands. Generally these women are seeking food, rather than seeking money, and receive pay in kind with an option of cash. Other women exchange weaving for money or corn.

In her research in K'at'ixtik, Diane Rus found that as wage work opportunities declined for men, and their family finances became more perilous, women—in addition to performing a multitude of labor intensive household duties such as grinding corn and making tortillas, hauling water and firewood, and weaving woolen clothes—began to search for additional jobs as well, however ill-paid, to preserve their families' tenuous hold on subsistence. In her survey of village women, she found that more than half produced embroidered shirts, woven bracelets, or some other handicraft for the tourist trade; performed piecework on handicrafts; gathered firewood to sell; made tortillas; or participated in field labor.

Most of these activities, Rus observed, brought in marginal incomes. Women sewing items that took one to two days to complete only earned around 1,500 [old] pesos (about $US 0.65) for a finished piece, an inordinately low sum when one considers that the minimum wage in Chiapas at the time was 7,000 pesos per day (about $US 3.00). For many women, however, piecework is the only option, according to Rus, because they lack the resources to buy the raw materials or feel that trying to sell their wares directly to stores in San Cristóbal de las Casas is too risky because the costs—the high price of transportation, the inability to communicate with Spanish-speaking shop owners, the possibility that no one will buy anything—outweigh the benefits. Women who worked as field hands or gathered firewood earned an even smaller pittance: 1,000 pesos per day and 1,500 to 3,000 pesos per week respectively. Chamula families in such circumstances are barely surviving, says Rus, who likens their living conditions to the days of serfdom on the *fincas* (large ranches and plantations).[6]

Gender and Generation Gaps

In contrast to the experiences of women, and older, poorer Zinacantecos, who continue to a certain extent to work for food, young men are hastening the change to a cash-based economy. Young men engaged in construction or other nonagricultural jobs expect to feed themselves, as do their Zinacanteco counterparts who run market stands or do trucking in distant lowland cities and towns. They relish sampling foods other than corn. And, ever attentive to style, they experiment with popular clothing, music, and electronic wares. As they bring new consumer goods home in the form of noncorn foods, faddish clothes, and even changed construction styles, youthful Zinacantecos are challenging the value that traditional villagers place on shared production and consumption of corn.

These conflicts emerge poignantly in marital disputes. In quarrels with their husbands, many women take their mates to task for spending their wages on nonessential goods such as soft drinks and radios rather than on corn and beans for their families. In disputes that pit young wives against their in-laws, the wives seek resolutions by setting up independent households through the division of corn supplies, even when their husbands earn most of their income in wage work and commerce. Young men often counter charges of neglect by pointing out new goods they have provided, such as the different kinds of footwear they have bought for their children (tennis shoes, plastic sandals, boots). And they sometimes try to resolve disputes through cash settlements. Family support, for them, does not center on provisioning their homes with corn, but, rather, with commodities bought from earnings.

In addition to creating conflicts between husbands and wives, the focus on wage work has contributed to a "generation gap" between young men and their elders. In the past, there was a general correlation of increasing age with wealth. But since 1981, this correlation has reversed. Young construction workers who learned skills and earned the wherewithal to undertake independent contracting, and young merchants who ventured forth into regional produce marketing, have catapulted ahead of many of their elders. Although wealthy elders with commercial enterprises of their own, especially truckers, continue to claim leadership within their communities, they increasingly find themselves confronted with "upstart" youths who contest their power. In Apas, this conflict was played out dramatically by young men who challenged the hegemony of the PRI-affiliated village elite by persuading a large faction of dissident peasants to join the rival Party of the Democratic Revolution (PRD). These militant youth, who flaunted the economic power of earnings from skilled construction and commerce, were challenging not just the party of their parents, but the long-standing collusion of village elders with the PRI.

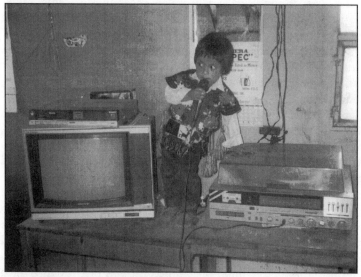

Photo 5.2 **New Consumer Goods.** A Zinacanteco trucker posed his son as a rock star amidst the electronic gear purchased with new wealth. Men sometimes spend earnings on such merchandise rather than on food and clothing needed by their families.

Even though many young men grew up in farming households, and contributed some of their labor to the milpa, their earned income has given them an unprecedented degree of independence. Because they do not draw on household corn supplies while away (selling or working), they justify contributing only a modest portion of their income, if any, to their parents. They feel free to spend their money on clothes—rancher-style boots, pants, hats—or, for that matter, on liquor, and sooner or later on marriage.

The economic independence of youth has drastically altered courtship and marriage in Apas. In the heyday of Zinacanteco milpa cultivation in the 1950s and 1960s, long and costly courtships were the rule, and suitors had to borrow from their parents to afford to marry, and to rely on elder kin to negotiate the marriage. Young couples began marriage heavily in debt, which they worked off by contributing their labor to the milpa production of the household in which they lived, usually that of the groom's parents. As the balance of power between parents and children has shifted, so have marriage practices. Today, many couples opt to elope, even though they know it will anger their parents, rather than participate in the expensive courtship rituals that will leave them penniless.

In the past, marriage brought the parents of the bride and groom into an alliance in which they held considerable power over their children's affairs, and their productive labor after marriage. Young couples had little recourse other than to parents for help in marital quarrels, intervention in disputes with neighbors, and assistance in rituals. Politics, in turn, revolved heavily, and often decisively, around the hold elders had over their married children. Such kin relations continue to be important today, but their tenor has shifted as other bases for power, class for example, have grown in importance. The changing economic conditions have not only refigured power relations within households, but within communities.

In Zinacantán, land ownership has shifted over the years to reflect the growing power of youth vis-à-vis their elder kin. When I surveyed farmland in 1967, 56 percent was in the hands of men over 45 years of age and only 35 percent was held by men aged 25–44 years. Today, by contrast, elder Zinacantecos control only 44 percent of the land, while men aged 25–44 hold 49 percent. This shift to young men is related to the changing age structure of the population, but it also mirrors young men's increasing economic independence and the concomitant advantages they have in transacting relations with elder kin. Many are unafraid to challenge parents and in-laws in the realm of public politics. And young adults can command the earlier distribution of inheritable assets as the price of supporting their parents in old age, rather than having to demonstrate the right to inheritance through respectful obedience.

The Widening Gap Between Rich and Poor

While *ejido* land itself has not yet become a commodity to be bought and sold, the use of land, to a great extent, had—even before the "reform" of Article 27 of the Constitution and the Agrarian Code liberalized the tenure and use of *ejido*. Firewood once free for women to gather anywhere in the *ejido* or communal lands is treated today as a private good to be bought and sold. Now that highland farming requires capital expenditures, poor families without assets more readily rent land to wealthier neighbors. During the 1987 farming season, the majority of those who rented out their land were single or widowed women "seeking" food in the form of rent in kind and poorer married men who made most of their living from work not requiring capital, as field hands or peons. Those who farmed rented land were wealthier young adults, many of whom derived substantial income from skilled wage work and commerce and who thus could afford fertilizer, weed sprays, and even the cost of farm laborers.

Renting farmland is one of the many alternatives, furthermore, in which Zinacantecos with cash can invest their assets flexibly. Rented land need not entail a long term commitment of renter to landowner. Thus Lorenzo De la Torre, a wealthy merchant and truck owner, rented enough Apas farmland in the 1987 season to employ as many as twenty-five field hands to work those fields for him; in 1989 he rented no land there having decided instead to farm land he had rented near lowland Villaflores, where he owns and runs his fruit and vegetable business. Such employers are often too deeply involved in activities other than farming to work alongside or directly supervise their workers. They may leave supervision to a dependent, or trust employees to work on their own. One Zinacanteco, Andrés Hernández, who works full-time in commerce, simply contracted the work of harvesting his milpa to three Zinacantecos as piece work to be paid a set amount regardless of how they organized the work.

Wealthy Zinacantecos whose small businesses give them cash to spare have come up with a nefarious new way of saving money: prepaying workers at a discount to contract for their future labor. Zinacantecos who are desperate for cash and cannot secure loans resort to selling their labor early, placing themselves at the disposal of their employer to call upon them when their labor is needed throughout the following agricultural cycle. In recent years, as wages have risen to adjust for inflation, the prepayment for future labor early in the agricultural cycle has been at about half the rate that prevails by the close of the cycle. For the employer, prepaying wages at a discount brings the wage down closer to the poor rate of return that milpa farmers receive on their own family labor, making it feasible for the employer to substitute hired labor for family labor. Such employment forces the worker to accept a low wage and strips him of the discretion to work for other employers later in the season except with the consent of the employer to whom he is indebted. The worker may even find himself assigned by his employer to work for someone else—a modern version of debt servitude!

Lending and borrowing have become more prevalent as Zinacantecos need more cash than ever before to farm milpa. Fertilizer and chemical weed sprays must be purchased, if not acquired on credit. Wages for field hands generally are paid in cash close to the time of work rather in kind from the future harvest. Truckers expect cash payment for transporting farmers to the field or harvest to market. Merchants need funds to purchase their inventory and cover transport and living costs while on selling trips. Zinacantecos who invest in such capital equipment as trucks or corn mills may resort to banks and government agencies for credits, but they also borrow from compatriots.

Before Salinas restructured the system of government agrarian credits and crop insurance, Zinacantecos who had rights in the *ejido* of Zinacantán or who owned communal land tracts were eligible for credit from the Banco Rural for the purchase of fertilizer with crop insurance from the National Agriculture and Livestock Insurance Program (ANAGSA). After Salinas's reforms, they still obtain credits available through the Solidarity program (discussed in Chapter 6). Farmers receive credit in June to pay off after harvest in February. Zinacantecos use these credits, especially if they lack cash in June when fertilizers need to be applied, but they feel penalized by having to repay credits in February at harvest time, when crop prices are at their seasonal low. Zinacantecos also borrowed significantly from one another, although at higher interest rates than offered by the Banco Rural, avoiding the paperwork loans require and the unfavorable date of maturity at harvest time.

Through lending, wealthy Zinacantecos are living in substantial measure from the surplus product of others' work in a manner that used to characterize only non-indigenous usurers. Their advantaged position enables some of them to explore new ways of living and working. A man nicknamed Jaguar, for example, age thirty-two, works less as a trucker today than when he ran both a truck and a van because he now earns interest on the money he made when he sold his van. He is reputed to have 20 million pesos out in loans. Unlike elders of yore who gathered followings by making loans to common folk, Jaguar lends only to men of substantial means. Jaguar still owns a truck, and he told me that he could easily earn one million pesos per month by running his truck every day. Instead, he runs his truck only on the weekdays that give him the most lucrative business because he earns so much income from interest.

Leaders Who No Longer Need Followers

In Chamula, political power for decades has been monopolized by a small group of indigenous caciques who received their mandate from the ruling party during the 1934–40 presidency of Lázaro Cárdenas, when they worked as scribes for government Indianist and labor organizers. With direct support from the PRI, their autocratic rule often serves the interests of the state rather than the citizens of Chamula, many of whom are unrecognized and unrepresented by the political system.[7] In Zinacantán, PRI-backed authorities have traditionally operated with a greater degree of accountability to their constituencies, but they are becoming more oppressive and elitist as a result of the economic changes brought by energy development.

As cash-based transactions have become more prevalent and young men challenge the traditional way of doing things, the social stratification of peasant communities has undergone tremendous change. Whole new classes of people—wealthy truckers, skilled masons, entrepreneurs—exist now and their prosperity has heightened the penury of the poorest sectors of peasant society and added a new complexity to productive relations. Those who have risen to the forefront of their communities in recent years exemplify different values and different styles of leadership than their predecessors.

Apas continues to be a place where people care deeply about protecting the integrity of indigenous life and *costumbre* against the amorality of the ladino world, Mexican law and the threat of

Protestantism and other nontraditional religions. But community members no longer agree on who has the authority to speak for traditional practices. Each political group claims a moral high ground, accusing others of collaborating with ladino politicians and lawyers. Instead of presenting a united front against the outside world, the differing factions have aligned themselves with national parties, and compete for control of state-allocated resources within their hamlets. Community members argue over who "belongs" in ethnic communities, and these arguments are exploited by local politicians to banish and exile their enemies. Apas has become a sharply divided community.

I believe that one of the reasons this is happening now is that in the post-oil boom society, where maintaining a group of followers is no longer necessary for political or economic ascendancy within peasant hamlets, it has become possible for leaders to act with an eye towards individual opportunity rather than community benefit. A primary distinction has emerged between people who sell their labor to others and those who undertake commercial ventures for themselves. The wealthy no longer have a need for webs of reciprocal obligations with the poor; the rank and file whose support they once cultivated have become expendable. Over the past twenty years, I have observed a shift from rank-based politics, in which politicians rose to power through a complex set of community obligations, to class-based politics, in which individuals use wealth as a route to power and prestige.

Think of rank-based power in relation to an economic system in which labor is the most important resource and advantage goes to those who can organize other people's services. One must demonstrate the ability to act effectively on others' behalf and be adept at pooling and channeling others' resources for both the personal and the common good. Rank-based leaders often serve their communities by acting as brokers with the outside world or as intermediaries to other groups, for example, by initiating a claim for land on behalf of their municipio. But first, of course, they must persuade others that they are worthy of being followed. They usually do so by competing with other would-be leaders to demonstrate who is the most willing to sacrifice personal well-being for the common good, often by undertaking ritual posts, which in the highlands of Chiapas are characteristically ranked in terms of cost and prestige.[8] The most effective contenders win respect and support, as well as deference and service, and finally the right to ask for others' resources to promote the common good. Even though they tend to do well by doing good in systems based on labor-intensive production, rank-based leaders usually play down differences in lifestyle from their followers while calling attention to the selfless service they give in leadership. Rank-based leaders epitomize those the Zapatistas laud as leaders who obey the will of their constituencies, who subordinate themselves to the needs of their followers.

Think of class-based power in relation to a system in which money is the most important resource and is used to purchase productive inputs, including the work of laborers who can be paid a wage without incurring other cumbersome obligations. In such a system, power holders use political positions to shepherd economic resources in a more exclusive manner, usually to better themselves at the expense of others, even if doing so means excluding others from access to wealth. Class-based leaders often have their power accorded to them from the state through positions from which they can garner benefit from state resources. Class-based leaders may unite with one another against their poor compatriots, the people that a rank-based leader would cultivate as followers.

The political careers of two prominent Apas men illustrate the shift from rank-based toward class-based politics that has taken place in Zinacantán and other communities. In the 1940s, Domingo Gerónimo won the support of Apas residents shortly after the initial distribution of *ejidal* land by insisting on egalitarian division of coffee groves near Ibestik, which other *ejidal* leaders had wanted to reserve for themselves. He represented Apas in the successful quest for additions to the *ejido* in the 1950s and pursued an impeccable career of service in Zinacantán's most costly religious posts. By orchestrating his followers and his kin to help fund the costly responsibilities of prestigious cargo positions, he gained the prerogative to speak for others. Community leaders during this period were more than politicians: they were called upon to settle disputes and preserve public civility by fostering feelings of interdependence and connectedness.

Gerónimo's son-in-law, Marcos Bromas, initially rose to power by following the same trajectory. He led the community in a long and ultimately successful effort to establish a lowland colony under the provisions of land reform, served as *ejidal* officer and also held a series of prestigious religious positions. He led his followers into the PAN in the late 1970s at a time when Zinacanteco leaders were beginning to make political party affiliations. But by the 1980s, Bromas, a truck driver who wanted to gain a route concession from the state, had begun to put his own interests before those of the community. He reached an agreement with other members of the new trucking elite and, disregarding the wishes of his followers, aligned himself with a powerful faction of the PRI—an action that turned many of his former supporters against him. In conversations about the situation, he admitted to me a certain weariness with the responsibilities of being a leader in the "old style" and expressed a desire for a more "pragmatic" system of politics without so many social obligations.

> I don't want to manage people any more. Let the municipal magistrate do what he's supposed to do and I'll support him. For I have tired of politics, not only party politics, but politicking for agrarian issues, for land . . .So that's how it came that there are [political] parties here. It was tied up with the trucks and the fact that we were quarreling with one another before. But today, we truckers are all in agreement.

Today, local leaders and politicians are much less likely to court the support of people they deem unimportant or powerless. They feel they have little stake in maintaining harmony among those who, in the previous era, would have been followers. For example, a young man recently approached a leader for help in resolving a domestic problem. His wife had been complaining that his elderly mother, who lived with them, was eating up too much food without contributing to the household income. Previously, it would have been the job of the leader to help the wife and mother come to some kind of accord, but in this case, the leader simply derided the older woman as a "rat who eats up all the corn of her children" and refused to get involved. He probably thought that since the chances of needing a favor from the woman were slim, she was not worth helping.

The shift from rank-based to class-based society is illustrated by many changes in individual and civic life. In the old days, economic relations were almost always subsumed in social ties. In return for political support, villagers expected to receive jobs to cover their subsistence. Leaders were careful to maintain roughly the same lifestyle as their followers. Today, it is not uncommon for economic relationships to remain purely economic—contracts can be made with strangers, and politicians feel little obligation to support the rank and file. In the past, politicians rose to power by amassing widespread popular support. Today they are most often powerful because Mexico's ruling party has supported them and given them control of public monies for their communities. As we shall see in the next chapter, such leaders may simply disdain to concern themselves with the poorer members of their communities.

As the gap between rich and poor widens, a complex set of variables comes into play. The lifestyle of rich and poor differs dramatically: the homes of the wealthy have tile roofs instead of thatch, and their dinners often include meat and chicken, luxuries the poor rarely taste. Studying the demography of Apas over the years, I have found that women and children in wealthy households now enjoy dramatically lower death rates than the poor, who suffer mortality comparable to the highest rates in the underdeveloped world. Peasants have restructured their communities by participating in a new range of activities, but they have also created strains that threaten to pull more and more people into a public arena marked by factionalism, conflict and inequality, and the breakdown of a web of mutual obligation that gave some protection to the poor.

The loss of traditional protections within communities comes at a time when government support, particularly rural subsidies, are also declining. As these protections erode, the very poorest people in Chiapas's highland villages have begun to fall out of the bottom strata of their communities into squatter settlements around cities, attempting to eke out a living from street vending or the sale of simple handicrafts.[9] The markets and commerce in the cities and larger towns of central and western Chiapas thus provide a safety valve for impoverished people. But in eastern Chiapas, which has no major commercial centers and is largely inaccessible even by road, the impoverished have had no place to turn and little to lose by joining the Zapatista rebellion.

The experience in the highlands underscores the risks as well as the opportunities inherent in the economic restructuring that

Mexican planners want for the rural economy and that peasants have already begun. Through changes in Article 27 of the Constitution and the Agrarian Code, Salinas and his advisors hope to further liberalize agrarian production. The changes legalize the sharecropping and the rental of *ejidal* lands that have taken place for years. But they also permit unprecedented privatization, mortgaging, the sale of *ejidal* parcels, and even of formerly undivided communal lands. They allow for outside investors to band together with peasants in joint ventures of commercial production based on the land. There is no question but that the liberalization of land tenure opens up opportunities for peasants to restructure agrarian production even more than they have already since 1982. But the liberalization also exposes poor and disadvantaged individual peasants to the unprecedented risk of losing land altogether to creditors. It thus removes one more protection for the poor.[10]

VI. EXCLUSION: THE NEW POLITICS

It is difficult to imagine what it would be like to live in a place where you could not enter the town hall, use the water system, seek redress for a crime committed against you, obtain a divorce, join in a community celebration, resolve a financial dispute or participate in a public project unless you were a member of a certain political party. But many towns in Chiapas have become just such places. Throughout Mexico's poorest state, access to public services is based not on need, but on political affiliation.

As support for the ruling party has begun to crumble, the PRI has increasingly turned to coercive tactics to hold on to the peasants' vote, withholding funds and services from those whose loyalty is suspect. Even in the tiniest hamlets of Chiapas, political "litmus tests" are used to determine who benefits from government programs and who does not.

These practices have produced sharply fractured villages where hostility reigns not just between Indian and ladino, but between pro-PRI Indian and anti-PRI Indian. Exclusionary politics have lent a new, divisive character to the political process in Chiapas's small Mayan towns, and social and economic changes tear at traditional community culture, heightening tensions between young and old, rich and poor, powerful and powerless.

These changes have created intense resentments that reinforce emerging class conflict within peasant communities. Those whom the ruling party favors gain privileged access to resources that should be available to everyone. Those who protest often find themselves locked out of the political process and, in some cases, expelled from their villages. Peasants have found numerous ways to express their dissent and reconfigure their communities, often forming their own parallel organizations when denied access to the government's, but they are also subject to increasing subtle and not-so-subtle repression.

In this chapter,[1] we follow the spread of such exclusionary politics into rural hamlets such as Apas, Zinacantán, continuing our case study of how the transformations that have occurred in Chiapas during the past decades of development and modernization have affected everyday life in the countryside. We examine the ways in which local indigenous leaders tacitly or explicitly collaborate with the PRI to stifle opposition, monopolizing government poverty funding for themselves and creating resentments of the same sort as those that have galvanized the Zapatista rebels to the east.[2]

"New Law," "New Politics"

For most of the past half century, the indigenous peasants of central Chiapas were loyal to the PRI. The ruling party put down strong roots among them in the 1930s when Lázaro Cárdenas instituted agrarian and labor reforms favoring Indians in central Chiapas and the Soconusco coast. Renewed agrarian reform and Indianist development solidified support for the ruling party in the 1950s, 1960s, and especially during the boom of the 1970s when the Mexican government was flushed with borrowed petrodollars. The ruling party had reason to take peasants' support for granted.

But the 1982 debt crisis forced the government to cut back on the programs that once bought peasant loyalty, and the government often turned to coercion or bribery to shore up support. Peasants, for their part, showed increasing independence and a greater propensity to join together to speak out against unacceptable policies.

In 1986, for example, the government suddenly raised the guaranteed price it would pay for corn by 32 percent—but only in the northern states, where several gubernatorial races were closely contested. The action backfired on two counts: it was widely interpreted as a blatant attempt to buy support for the PRI candidates, and it infuriated southern farmers, who did not benefit from the price increase.

Peasants in Chiapas responded swiftly, deriding the government's actions and demanding that corn prices be increased across the board. A coalition of corn producers organized public protests, rallying in Tuxtla Gutiérrez and blocking roads when their demands went unheeded. On January 17, 1986, Chiapas Governor

Absalón Castellanos Domínguez sent troops to repress a widely publicized blockade of the Pan American highway near Ixtapa, jailing even bystanders and newspaper reporters who were covering the event. Some of those arrested languished in jail for over two years, a violation of basic human rights and due process.

The incident underscored the state's willingness to use coercive measures to keep its constituency in line, a lesson that was not lost on the indigenous peoples of the highlands. But the protests also demonstrated that the government could no longer take loyalty from the peasants of Chiapas for granted.

After the closely contested 1988 presidential elections, which opposition parties claimed were stolen for Carlos Salinas de Gortari, the PRI stepped up its policing of peasant loyalty. When José Patrocinio González Garrido, a PRI-ista, took office as the new Governor of Chiapas in 1988, he revised the penal code to make it easier for the state government to punish dissent. Referred to as the "new law" in peasant communities, the penal code established González as a hard liner.[3]

Article 13 of Governor González's new law concerned "unruly crowds" and outlined penalties for those who lead, organize, incite, or support "mob" action. Article 120 criminalized as "rebellion" against the government the actions of anyone who interferes with the function of state institutions or elections. Article 135 penalizes those in "mobs" or "riots" deemed to disturb public order or menace public functionaries or authorities on the pretext of exercising a legal right. Article 336 made it illegal to invade property for purposes of appropriation or profit. On its face, this provision seems reasonable—until one takes into account that peasant invasion of lands taken away from them by ranchers is sometimes the only way peasants can reclaim land under the provisions of agrarian reform.

Taken together, these provisions empowered the Chiapas government to quell spontaneous public protest, curb organized opposition, and restrain agrarian activists. According to human rights jurists who criticized Chiapas's penal code,[4] "[t]he provisions, taken together, . . . create[d] broad categories of political crimes which embrace[d] every conceivable form of political protest, with the possible exception of the printed word." Put into practice, the penal code "filled [Chiapas's] prisons with political prisoners."

The Chiapas government's implementation of the new law also stripped local non-PRI leaders of their authority. Since colonial times, local authorities in indigenous communities have been allowed to resolve all non-felony disputes among families and neighbors according to indigenous customary law. Resolving disputes has been one of the responsibilities of each township's elected president, whose administrative functions are similar to those of a mayor. Each township also has judges, and hamlets have magistrates who use customary law to resolve local problems.[5] Beginning in the 1970s, when political factions began to divide hamlets, each faction was allowed its own magistrate, school committee representatives, local tax collectors, and so forth. Thus, in 1988, both the PRI faction in Apas and an opposing faction that called themselves the *Campesinos* had their own magistrates and local magistrate office. This ensured that people need not rely on someone from a rival political faction to settle their disputes.

This all changed in 1989. The Chiapas government decreed that only one magistrate per hamlet would be allowed and that magistrates had to hold an official appointment from the governor. Because Governor González's appointments for Zinacantán were all in the PRI, only PRI magistrates held legitimate office, leaving people in other factions without their own legal recourse to customary law. When opposition factions complained in Zinacantán Center, PRI town authorities pointedly warned that the new law could be used against anyone who challenged the PRI. The municipal president summoned the magistrates of each hamlet to the town hall and announced his intention to weed out the non-PRI representatives:

> There is only one President of the Republic. There is only one state governor. There is only one municipal president. Why should hamlets be the only place where there is more than one chief authority?

In Apas, where twice as many families aligned themselves with the Campesinos as with the PRI, this new policy outraged the Campesinos. Several days after the decision not to authorize faction magistrates, the two factions argued and came to blows. Some of the local PRI authorities were injured and accused the Campesinos of having plotted against them. The municipal president summoned the Campesinos and warned them not to assault

PRI representatives again because the new law now allowed those who acted against authorities to be jailed without the possibility of bail. The municipal secretary then questioned the Campesinos closely as to whether or not they belonged to an opposition party. The Campesinos replied that no, they were simply a division within the PRI. Under the new law, the secretary warned them, opposition to established authorities of the PRI could be punished. He told them that "as a favor" he would write up an official account of the ruckus as merely as a dispute between two "groups," but that in the future the Campesinos could be charged as an illegal opposition group. In effect, Zinacantecos were being told that by opposing local PRI authorities, they were opposing the government itself and could be arrested.

Shortly afterward, several hamlets sent a delegation of Campesino faction members to the state capital to appeal the ruling on magistrates and gain recognition of their own. Although they claimed to be a group within the PRI, Governor González refused to recognize them on this basis. Four months later, Apas's Campesinos gave up any pretense of affiliation with the PRI by joining the Cardenistas—followers of Cuauhtémoc Cárdenas in the Party of the Democratic Revolution (PRD)—in part because a PRD state congressman promised them support in winning recognition of their own magistrate. But once again the governor refused them the magistrate they needed for recourse to customary law.

Shortly thereafter, in the nearby hamlet of Nachih, Cardenistas staged a PRD rally. Violence broke out when PRI local authorities roughed up and jailed several Cardenistas, including Margarito Ruiz Hernández, a PRD deputy to the federal congress who should have enjoyed constitutional immunity from arrest. After protest of the incident, which attracted national publicity because of the flagrant violation of Ruiz Hernández's immunity, the state government pledged to bring the errant PRI-istas to justice. The governor deposed two of the hamlet's PRI authorities, but charges of wrongdoing were eventually dropped for "lack of evidence," indicating that the government would look the other way when PRI militants used violence against the opposition.

Control of Money

In addition to making public protest illegal, the government also used subtle financial controls to ensure that local opposition leaders would never be able to administer public funds. This was another way of disempowering opponents while reserving the opportunity to profit from public funding for PRI loyalists. The government exerted pressure on individuals to toe a party line, withholding permission to operate private enterprise unless the principals involved belong to the PRI. The two anecdotes below illustrate this combination of political and financial discrimination and favoritism.

In 1982, the democratically elected president of Zinacantán, Pedro Vásquez, went to the town hall to assume his position. Instead of a welcoming committee or a celebration, Vásquez, a member of the PAN party, found locked doors, barred windows, and a group of local PRI leaders. They told him that he could not enter the building because it was built with PRI labor and owned by the PRI. Vásquez appealed to the governor, who told local authorities that they had no choice but to allow him into the town hall. After Vásquez took office, however, the state used its power over the municipal budget to persuade Vásquez to leave the PAN and join the PRI. The stakes were substantial because the state government, since 1980, had made a practice of providing block grants to municipal authorities to fund public works, putting control of projects directly in their hands. Zinacanteco factions began to align with national political parties to compete for control of this money.[6]

At around the same time, Marcos Bromas, a prominent Apas citizen (see previous chapter), was also persuaded to leave the PAN and join the PRI. Bromas had been a major leader of the PAN in Zinacantán and had stood for election to the state congress as a PAN candidate. But when Bromas, head of a trucker's union, tried to get a route concession from the state—something he could not operate without—he realized that it would be impossible given his party affiliation. Bromas told me,

> We went to a meeting at PRODESCH [the government's regional development agency] where the lawyers urged us to drop the other party (PAN) and put an end to politics. They tried to convince us that it would be best for the whole of

Zinacantán to be of just one party. I said I would agree, for they had told me that otherwise, getting my route authorized would be difficult.

During the 1982–88 presidency of Miguel de la Madrid, Mexico struggled under a stringent austerity program imposed by the international banking community. The federal government lost the option of trying to cull support by wholesale funding of public projects. In Chiapas, outgoing governor Absalón Castellanos Domínguez emptied state coffers in 1988, leaving the state government without funds even to pay year-end salaries of teachers. Neither government was in a position to use public money to coopt support.

When Patrocinio González Garrido became governor, he shrewdly sidestepped the lack of funding by holding out the *promise* of state money. Without actually earmarking any money for specific projects, he offered Indians a larger role in planning public expenditures. He reorganized the state agencies responsible for Indian affairs under a new State Indigenous Council in 1989, to which he gave authority over state projects for indigenous communities. Officially, the purpose of the Council was to "involve Indians in the solution of their own problems, such as the protection of their rights, without paternalism."[7] Each indigenous community sent one of its authorities as a representative to the council.

By establishing the Council, Governor González deferred real funding for Indian affairs projects. Because the PRI controlled all but two of the state's 111 town halls, the representatives sent to the Council were virtually all of the PRI. That ensured that the council could channel government funding to PRI initiatives when funding eventually became available.

Zinacantecos were never in doubt about the intensely political character of public funding, before or after the establishment of the Council. In Apas, politics centered on the use and abuse of public funding. Addressing the Campesino dissidents to persuade them to become Cardenistas at a rally in Apas on April 9, 1989, a lawyer from Tuxtla Gutiérrez representing the PRD spoke in Spanish of the new party's project:

> What is our program? It is a book that perhaps you know. Our program cost one million lives in 1910. Our program is the *Constitución Mexicana*. It says that every Mexican has a right

to land, but that right has not been recognized; we intend to recognize it. It gives people the right to health, but this is not honored; we will honor it. The Constitution grants workers a salary adequate for food, clothing, and housing, which workers don't have. And here in Chiapas, which produces electricity that's even exported to other countries of Central America, here thousands of families lack electricity.

Chiapas has great wealth, but it's the Governors who exploit it, along with PRI officials. Chiapas's wealth doesn't go to all of us, but rather to just a few. And just a handful of millionaires get the wealth; those are the people who join the PRI, because in doing so they know they will be allowed to rob. For the PRI encourages them to be one another's accomplices. Thus when municipal presidents leave office, their successors don't do audits, they know that they will be able to act in their own right for their own benefit. All of them are hiding under the same blanket. But the nation will no longer stand for it.

Claiming that the PRI had stolen the 1988 presidential elections, the PRD lawyer urged the Zinacantecos to form a PRD committee in Apas to prepare for future elections and to channel local requests for immediate public support to state agencies with PRD assistance:

Without anyone to support you, you are vulnerable to the authorities robbing you without solving any of your problems. But the PRD will help you. If you need potable water, if you need a clinic, school, or kindergarten, you can draw up a request with many signatures and we will help you go to the Presidencia Municipal [town hall] or to Tuxtla.

One of the new Apas Cardenista militants, nicknamed Master Mason because of the skills he learned in construction work, took the stand, ostensibly to paraphrase in Tzotzil what the visitor had said. But where the lawyer had voiced the PRD's general appeal to peasants and workers for land, wages, and social justice and had spoken against PRI electoral fraud and graft, Master Mason emphasized government aid and charged that Zinacanteco municipal authorities of the PRI—the trucker elite—corruptly enriched themselves by stealing funds intended for the hamlets:

Photo 6.1 **Organizing Rally for the Party of the Democratic Revolution (PRD) in Zinacantán.**

The lawyer criticized the way the PRI conducted elections in Zinacantán, and how those who have held office all leave office with trucks and possessions. It's not just the Ladinos who are thieves . . . . The lawyer spoke of the past municipal presidents as thieves. One of them is in jail in Cerro Hueco [the state penitentiary in Tuxtla] for having stolen 20 million pesos. Although that money was supposed to be assistance to the *pueblo*, the President enriched himself. He didn't give out the aid to each hamlet. This is not just a story, it has come out in the newspaper and on the radio. That's the way the PRI really works. It's not like someone just stealing corn on the cob, or stealing some peaches, its not just a few thousand pesos, rather it's more like 100 million pesos that they stole.

But now that this new party is here, they can help us scrutinize what happens with each kind of assistance that is supposed to come to our hamlets. For example, we don't have water, we have to work hard hauling water. If we don't have wells of our own, we have to get water from people who do. But with this here party, then we can really get *agua potable* [a water system]. And so with a clinic. We don't have a clinic of our own. We have to go to San Cristóbal to be treated, and when we do we aren't really helped. Here again the Cardenista party can help us. It is not that they are going to give us aid directly, but rather that they will help us ask the government for aid. What we have to do is tell the party what it is that we need, and then they will help us ask for it.

Not all of Apas's dissidents were eager to follow Master Mason and other militants into the PRD. Elders were the most skeptical. Campesinos were, for the most part, poorer hamlet members among whom elders had achieved social status by years of civil and religious service. The militants, by contrast, were young men of new wealth who, like Master Mason, had learned construction skills in the 1970s and had gone into contracting or commerce in the 1980s. By inviting the Campesinos to join the PRD, these young militants were mounting a double challenge, to elders of their own faction and to the PRI elite in Zinacantán Center and Apas, led by truckers such as Marcos Bromas. By joining the PRD, which posed as the party of peasants and workers that would bring benefits such as health clinics and water systems to all citizens, the young militants deflected attention away from their own new wealth. After a second PRD rally in late April, attended by the

PRD state deputy Jorge Moscoso Pedrero, the elders reluctantly followed the militants into the Cardenista party.

As we have seen, the ruling party refused to grant Apas Cardenistas their own magistrate. The PRI also sabotaged Cardenista initiatives for public projects.

Shortly after joining the PRD, Apas Cardenistas submitted an orchard and water project proposal to CONAFRUT, the agricultural extension agency that funded orchard projects. They proposed to plant fruit trees and repair Apas's damaged and long-unused water system so that it could supply drinking water and water for new orchards. When Zinacanteco PRI authorities learned of the proposal, they had their representative to the State Indigenous Council, which monitored CONAFRUT projects, kill the Cardenista proposal. They persuaded the Apas PRI faction to submit a proposal of their own, requesting only trees. When I visited Apas in December 1989, the CONAFRUT seedlings had arrived—the only public project approved for Apas in 1989—and the PRI-istas were planting them. The ruling party had cut off Cardenista access to scarce state funding.

Tradition Versus Literacy and Law

Even as Zinacantecos and other indigenous peasants incorporate changes in agriculture and politics into their traditional villages, they continue to think of themselves as Indians. But new alignments of class and power are jeopardizing disadvantaged peoples' rights to belong to their ethnic communities.

Despite the changes in their lives, Zinacantecos continue to think of themselves as people whose morality, as embodied in *costumbre,* is superior to that of nonindigenous Mexicans—even though non-Indians hold secular power in the world at large. For Zinacantecos and other indigenous groups, tradition shapes the logic of the familiar ethnic world, whereas literacy and law govern the alien ladino world which exercises power over Indians.

Tzotzil until recently was an unwritten language. Because most Indians are monolingual and illiterate and most ladinos are literate and Spanish-speaking, Zinacantecos link literacy to the power that ladinos have over Indians. As Master Mason put it after translating for the PRD lawyer at the first Cardenista rally:

>That's more or less what the ladino lawyer said, as far as I understood it. And you others can add from what you understood. For not all of us know how to read and write. If we did, then we could be thieves like the ladinos living in cities, in San Cristóbal and Tuxtla, rather than working as we do with our machetes. They just want to sit in offices and eat off of that.

Literacy confers the power to "eat" off of those who work with their machetes, especially in the case of those who can use reading to avail themselves of the power of law.

Indians sometimes turn to ladino law, however, to use its repressive power against fellow Indians. When Don Andrés's son Manuel quarreled with his father over land and threatened him, Andrés told him to get out of the house. "Fine," said Manuel, "I'll leave. But I am going to get myself a lawyer in San Cristóbal to get the land for myself." Manuel's threat to go to a lawyer is what Zinacantecos who have anger in their hearts do to make trouble. Rather than seeking settlement by appealing to traditional authorities within the community, those who turn to ladino lawyers can have the lawyers slap their opponents with litigation fees, fines, bribes, and punitive jail terms—the repressive tools of domination.

Lawyers, as far as Indians are concerned, are the ones who connect literacy and law to the power that ladinos hold over Indians. From the time of President Lázaro Cárdenas onward, government agency lawyers have controlled and manipulated indigenous politics. INI and PRODESCH lawyers always worked behind the scenes to guarantee that compliant PRI leaders would hold municipal offices. When Marcos Bromas and other PAN-istas succumbed to pressure to return to the PRI in 1982, PRODESCH lawyers were the ones to press them.

Now, as the rank-based politics of consensus succumb to the new class-based politics of party, Zinacantecos have begun to use wealth to compete in politics and have even turned to the alien world of law to make trouble for opposing political factions. They often do so in the name of tradition.

Indigenous communities in the Chiapas highlands began splitting into factions affiliated with outside political parties in the late 1970s. They simultaneously adhered to *costumbre* by competing with one another in ritual performance, each group trying to prove that it was more "Zinacanteco" than the others. Factions collected fiesta taxes separately, forcing every household to chose a side. Opposing factions hired rival bands to play for their members at fiestas and sponsored rival fireworks displays and processions. Apas Cardenistas lament what they characterize as the demise of costumbre in the customary law administered by PRI authorities in Zinacantán Center. "It used to be that you could get the President to settle a case with a bottle of liquor," the Cardenistas complain. "But now so much money is involved because of the way the authorities are using the new law." Instead of trying to quiet anger in litigants' hearts in the traditional way, by getting them to drink together to acknowledge settlement, the Cardenistas charge, the president imposes fines in the manner of the ladino judiciary. The PRI officials argue in rebuttal that they try their best to settle litigation "by *costumbre*," that opposition litigants like the Cardenistas are the ones who throw tradition to the winds by using outside lawyers and legal maneuvers.

Most town hall litigation no longer involves the proffer of liquor to calm antagonists' hearts, as once it invariably did. What has changed, I believe, is not that offering and accepting liquor has ceased to signify heart-felt casting away of anger, but rather that politicians no longer care to bring fights to resolution. Instead, they often show disdain for people seeking their help—as if others' problems are too petty to be bothered with. Previously, politicians had a stake in settling things amicably; they wanted litigants to depend on them and help bolster their positions in the community. Now, unless the litigant is powerful or wealthy, local PRI politicians are simply not interested, because their power rests now in control of capital and public monies, not in retinues of followers.[8]

As a result, those who oppose the PRI lose customary access to reconciliation of debts, marital disputes, quarrels over child support—the very problems that agrarian change and the increasing differentiation of poor and wealthy have sharpened.

When Don Andrés's sister Lorenza begged him to accompany her to Zinacantán Center in 1989 to help her divorce her husband, Andrés's refusal called attention to her isolation, as a Cardenista, from ordinary recourse to traditional justice. Lorenza had to go to Zinacantán Center, the lowest judicial level at which municipal authorities have jurisdiction over divorce. But Lorenza's husband was one of the Cardenistas in Apas. Even though Andrés is a hamlet-level PRI authority, he could not assure her that she would receive a fair hearing in Zinacantán Center. Andrés told me what he had said to his sister, advising her to ask their brother, Mariano, a Cardenista, to help her instead:

> "Look, Lorenza, it isn't my affair. If I were a Cardenista, then, sure, I'd go with you to Zinacantán Center, but I'm PRI," I said. "But the Cardenistas don't go to Zinacantán Center. Who knows where they go to settle their problems, perhaps Tuxtla, perhaps elsewhere," I said.

> "But I want to give him up for good," said Lorenza [referring to her husband]. "What use is it to me to be living in the same house with him?"

> "Do whatever you want. If you want to break up, fine. I'm not going to tell you to leave your husband."

> "But Mariano [Lorenza's Cardenista brother] doesn't want to go to Zinacantán Center," she replied.

> "Why not?"

> "Who knows?"

> "Well, I don't want to go either," Andrés said, "for I know that the authorities will ask me if you are from the PRI, and I will have to tell them you and your husband are Cardenistas. Then they're likely to say 'Who knows what municipio the Cardenistas belong to?' And that won't do."

Taunting the Apas Cardenistas repeatedly with the query, "Where is your President, where is your municipio?," the hamlet's PRI minority were insinuating that Cardenistas deserve exile.

The threat to exile fellow Zinacantecos because of their politics is not dissimilar to the exile other highland groups suffer on religious grounds. Exile is just what "Protestants"—often simply dissidents or disaffected poor—are experiencing at the hands of power holders in many Tzotzil and Tzeltal communities as the strains of agrarian change ripple through the landscape. Chamula, which we have discussed in comparison to Zinacantán as a neighboring township more sharply and adversely differentiated by agrarian changes, has become notorious for the action taken by its PRI-affiliated political leaders against thousands of citizens forced into exile since the early 1970s on the pretext of religious affiliation. During 1989 alone, hundreds of indigenous families were expelled from Oxchuc, Mitontic, Amatenango del Valle, and Chenalhó, ostensibly as Protestants.[9] Zinacantán has also exiled Protestant converts, although in far fewer numbers than has Chamula. The exiles join others who have taken up refuge in squatter settlements that have grown up around San Cristóbal as a result of economic and political adversity, rather than simply religious antagonism.

For generations, Zinacantecos have embraced costumbre, as both the Cardenistas and the PRI-istas in Apas still claim to do. They have defended the integrity of their place in the world as an ethnic community. In a new era of exclusionary politics, will powerful Zinacantecos go so far as to deprive poor compatriots of their ethnic citizenship? Will PRI-istas attempt to cast out the Cardenistas? Before the Zapatista uprising, that seemed like a possibility.

Divided Solidarity

In 1988, six years after the debt crisis forced austerity and restructured the Mexican economy, PRI candidate Carlos Salinas de Gortari claimed the presidency on the basis of elections that many—both Mexicans and non-Mexicans—believed had been stolen from the opposition.

Scholars of Mexican politics[10] wondered whether Mexico could continue to liberalize its economy without modernizing its political system. Budget cuts had gutted many of the government programs that helped the ruling party secure popular support and middle-class standards of living had declined. Some kind of partial democratization or political liberalization seemed advisable to prevent a disgruntled populace from joining with opposition groups to force a political change.

Salinas, upon taking office, set a course that seemed to move in the direction of political liberalization. He revised Article 41 of the Constitution and established two federal entities to reform elections: an electoral institute to register voters, prepare elections, and oversee public tabulation of votes; and an electoral tribunal to adjudicate electoral disputes. He also declared amnesty for many who had been jailed for their involvement in social and political battles, and set up a National Human Rights Commission to monitor human rights violations. Salinas took highly publicized and popular actions by arresting strongmen in the powerful oil worker's union (Joaquín Hernández Galicia, nicknamed "La Quina"), in the securities market (Eduardo Legorreta Chauvet), and in the drug trade (Miguel Angel Félix Gallardo) on charges of corruption.[11]

With much fanfare, Salinas also launched a national antipoverty program called Solidarity (PRONASOL, which is administered under the Ministry of Social Development, SEDESOL) to ameliorate the hardships posed by economic restructuring for the nation's poor—the 48 percent of the population who lived below the official poverty line in 1988. Under austerity and in the name of economic restructuring, the government phased out important benefits for Mexico's poor including price controls, and subsidies for basic foods such as tortillas. It also removed subsidies for peasant agriculture and disbanded state-run institutions such as INMECAFE that served peasant producers. Solidarity began to channel funds into five areas: food subsidies for specifically targeted low-income groups; credits for poor farmers engaged in high-risk production; development projects in indigenous communities; social programs to improve access to clinics and schools; and infrastructure such as electricity and water systems for low-income rural and urban homes. As restructuring reduced public funding for social programs through other channels, Solidarity gained prominence by funneling as much as 1.08 percent of Mexico's gross domestic product into these initiatives in 1992.[12]

Solidarity officials, Salinas announced, would collaborate with communities to develop what might be thought of as co-participative programs based on community initiatives, joint responsibility, and honest administration of resources, without regard to participants' political affiliations. The program epitomized what Salinas hoped his administration would achieve by way of *concertación* or consensus building across the political spectrum. Salinas wanted Solidarity to:

> eliminate all vestiges of paternalism, populism, clientelism, or political conditionality in the improvement of the welfare of the population in poverty . . . . The activities carried out under the National Solidarity Program represent an

> investment in physical and social welfare infrastructure that
> *by their very nature* promote justice and democracy.[13]

Solidarity resources were primarily distributed outside the framework of the ruling party, bypassing traditional power holders in favor of new political actors and institutions. Taken at face value, Solidarity seemed to open up more democratic access to state resources. Coupled with electoral and human rights initiatives, Solidarity looked like the start of a whole new era of government.

Why, then, did Solidarity fail to win popular support in Chiapas, which as one of Mexico's poorest states received more Solidarity funding than any other state in the country?

One reason is that Solidarity funding came too little and too late to ease the hardships that economic restructuring brought to the agrarian sector. One goal of Solidarity in Chiapas was to assist the small producers of coffee who had lost their money and their livelihoods when INMECAFE, the Mexican National Coffee Institute, was disbanded.

During the 1980s, INMECAFE had given peasants credits to purchase fertilizer and other inputs for growing coffee, and had guaranteed a market for their crop. Large commercial plantations grow coffee in the Soconusco region of Chiapas, but so do peasants on *ejidos* and small holdings there and in the central and eastern parts of the state, where the Union of Unions (UU) won marketing concessions from INMECAFE in 1980. In most regions, INMECAFE tended to favor peasants organized into *ejidal* unions affiliated with the PRI's national peasant confederation, the National Peasant Confederation (CNC). It also dictated the terms for these unions' production.[14]

After Salinas disbanded INMECAFE as part of his program to get the national government out of state-run enterprises, his Solidarity program targeted small coffee producers in Chiapas to ease the hardships posed by the collapse of world coffee prices in 1989. Solidarity gave credits to individuals organized within local Solidarity committees and provided some support for marketing. But Solidarity could support only the most impoverished of coffee producers, and for most peasants, the program's assistance was inadequate, according to one expert appraisal:

> Has [Solidarity] been successful in combatting extreme
> poverty in the coffee sector? In the 1989–90 season, a small

producer with two hectares in coffee, producing a crop of 500 lbs., earned the equivalent of 369 days of work at the minimum wage. In 1991–92, that same producer earned the equivalent of 195 days of work at the minimum wage. Thus, the answer must be "no". Small coffee producers are poorer today than when Solidarity began. Clearly [Solidarity] is not to blame for this situation, though it did not prevent it either. It is true that, given the withdrawal of INMECAFE, without [Solidarity] things would be worse. But the situation is, nevertheless, far from good.[15]

A more telling criticism of Solidarity is that its implementation in Chiapas did not honor the program's promise to hand out funding without regard to the political affiliation of its recipients. Solidarity channeled substantial support to indigenous peasants in Chiapas through the National Indian Institute (INI), which set up regional councils of indigenous representatives to formulate strategic projects.[16] At first it appeared as though INI-sponsored initiatives would actually reach out to indigenous and peasant groups regardless of their political affiliation. But in 1992, Chiapas governor Patrocinio González Garrido arrested and jailed three top INI officials in Chiapas on what many believed to be trumped-up charges of corruption. Critics maintained that the governor was angry that INI was dispensing Solidarity funds to PRI opposition in independent peasant groups in eastern Chiapas.[17] After the governor put his own people in charge of INI, the agency's Solidarity program once again became an instrument for ruling party clientelism.[18] In Zinacantán, for example, Cardenistas lost Solidarity's support for a community project after new directors took charge at INI in 1992.

INI's administration of Solidarity also fell short of the program's commitment to aid grassroots initiatives without paternalism. Indigenous representatives complained about this failing during an August 1993 meeting convoked by INI in San Cristóbal de las Casas.

A video of the meeting made by one of the indigenous representatives calls attention to subtle paternalism inherent in the very organization of the meeting. With one exception, the high-ranking officials who led the meeting were nonindigenous men. The women of INI's nonindigenous staff were given responsibility for running the workshops. The organizers relegated indigenous staff and indigenous representatives to the audience in plenary sessions, and to roles in workshops that to my eye treated them like school children, seating them around tables to write their ideas with colored pens on paper posters to put up on the blackboard under the supervision of the INI staff members. My own impression is that such paternalism is so deeply embedded in Mexico's treatment of Indians that those who exercise it are not always conscious of the resentment paternalism engenders—resentment that the Zapatistas voiced through Juan, one of the delegates to the February 1994 peace negotiations:

> We fight to gain respect for our dignity . . . . What offends us most is the inability to express our sentiments, our demands. Let it be clear that we fight for our dignity as Indians and so that we will not be stigmatized . . . . For years we have not been respected . . . . We say this in order that we stop being sold like animals in a zoo, so that we get treated as persons and humans.[19]

An indigenous representative at the August 1993 INI meeting angrily voiced his criticisms of INI's Solidarity programs in one of the workshops, urging compatriots to reject INI's paternalistic and heavy-handed management:

> We can't let them tell us what to do and what not to do, comrades. Those bastards treat us as though to say, "You, Indians, sit down and keep quiet . . . ." We've heard from one another how we're told to run things at our own initiative but then not allowed to do so. They want us to do things only the INI way.

> The fact is that our enemies control the different institutions, such as INI, right now. They've decided to support Indians, or, you might say, to put up with the scourge of the Indians, but what kind of relation to the state can we really enter into?

Like Zinacantecos in Apas, and Zapatistas who accuse public officials of merely using Indians as a stepping stone to positions of advantage and power, he complained that bureaucrats were using literacy and legalism to take advantage of Indians:

> For two days we've shown that we know how to work, how to get things done. Sure, we have setbacks, we have delays, but we're also making progress. I think that shows that we Indians are real *chingones* [studs/fuckers], that we know how to survive even on our few grains of corn. Why, then, won't they let us keep on making progress?

It's because we have trouble doing the paperwork. Now they want us to fill out all these forms. If we don't do all the paperwork, they won't give us the money. The money's there. But if you don't know how to fill out the paperwork, then you have to give all the money back . . . .

The truth is that the staff secretaries don't want to do the work. The truth is that not all of the INI employees are hard workers, many of them want to be there behind a desk, just like other functionaries.

You gentlemen, [he said, addressing the INI officials,] help us. We need your support and your advice. But we don't want your impositions. We don't want you to tell us our projects are no good, but rather to help us strengthen our projects. You have to realize that the projects we propose are not our personal projects, not something dreamed up by just anyone, but rather by our public assemblies . . . .

We [peasants] have been working on these projects for just three years, comrades. Think about it. For seventy years, *they* say, they've been trying to help Indians. But they haven't been able to make any progress, they haven't found the right shot, the right pill to cure the Indians' poverty. And here we are, wanting to progress, willing to work, and now they change the accounting system on us, after seventy years of perpetrating abuses and robbing money from the poor.

At which point, the conference organizers interrupted to shut this man up.

Perhaps the most important shortcoming of Solidarity administration in Chiapas was that the majority of its support was administered directly through municipal governments, virtually assuring that its benefits would flow to supporters of the ruling party, and not to opponents. The ostensible purpose of administering Solidarity funds through municipalities was to encourage locally planned initiatives. But in Chiapas, where the ruling party has deposed virtually every opposition candidate who has won a town hall presidency, block grants to municipalities have perpetuated and sharpened the subtle and not so subtle politics of exclusion that we have seen at work in Zinacantán. In Zinacantán, PRI authorities used Solidarity funding to build a grandiose new municipal hall, one of several public building projects that primarily benefitted the truckers paid to transport the construction materials. Not surprisingly, in the wake of the Zapatista rebellion, other Zinacantecos have begun to hold the PRI authorities accountable for purported misappropriation of the public works funding.

In the central highlands of Chiapas, the politics of exclusion seemed to have worked for the PRI up to the moment of the Zapatista uprising. Now, as Mexicans contemplate the seeming debacle of Salinas de Gortari's triumphalist modernizing, and as peasant and indigenous groups throughout Mexico are acknowledging the legitimacy of Zapatista grievances, it appears that the PRI has gravely jeopardized its ability to hold on to power, in Chiapas or elsewhere, without radically reconsidering the nation's goals.

Shortly after the Zapatista's January 1, 1994, uprising, opposition groups in dozens of municipalities in Chiapas seized town halls to protest the purportedly corrupt practices of PRI authorities imposed on many municipalities by the ruling party. These protests within communities are understandable when one considers that the politics of exclusion spread throughout the Mexican countryside under the tenure of state governors such as Patrocinio González Garrido.

Analysts on the left of the political spectrum[20] argue that the Mexican bourgeois state, by stirring up factionalism among the peasantry, has been able to make class contradictions in Mexican society—between those who own the means of production and those whom production exploits—seem to disappear. Conflicts that have roots in fundamental inequalities separating peasants from large landowners, they say, have been written off as "Indian problems." I think there is merit to the claim that the ruling party has fostered factionalism in the peasantry in order to divide and rule in the Mexican countryside. But I also believe it is important not to overlook how such tactics resonate with and sharpen the class divisions fostered within peasant society by energy development and agrarian change in Zinacantán and throughout Mexico's southeast.

In this light, the Zapatista rebellion becomes understandable as a response to the growing differentials between rich and poor, and between favored and excluded groups within the rural society of Chiapas. We can better understand why the Zapatistas feel betrayed by peasant groups within the Union of Unions or the ARIC, which have accepted ruling party patronage and commercial support and, consequently, have been criticized for selling out their compatriots. But above all, we know that the conflict in Chiapas arises directly from a quarter of a century of Mexican development and modernization, and that solutions must take this into account.

VII. TRANSITIONS AND PROSPECTS

The weeks before the August 21, 1994 Mexican presidential elections were a time of great anxiety within Mexico about the country's immediate future, given the prospect that the ruling party might not credibly win the vote.

> The problem is that not even once in this country's recent history—not since 1911—has power been transferred by means of elections. Never. There is no tradition of that here whatsoever. None. None. None at all!

This, said Jorge G. Castañeda, a prominent Mexican political scientist, was why he and some forty members of the so-called "San Angel" group, named after the district in Mexico City where many politicians, intellectuals, and social leaders live, had been discussing privately how to ward off a political crisis that could accompany the elections.[1]

Modern Mexicans cannot look to a precendent for a model for a peaceful transfer of power from the ruling party in the event of a loss. There has been no transfer of power since the 1910–1920 Revolution and opposing parties have never held office. In what has become institutionalized as the *dedazo*, PRI leaders transfer power by "fingering" their candidate for the next elections at the end of each six-year presidential term.

While the 1994 elections were relatively free of violence, many Mexicans are looking back to the 1910–1920 Revolution itself for ways of imagining how a change of government might someday take place. The last *change* in the Mexican government came after the 1911 elections in which Madero forced six-term president and virtual dictator Porfirio Díaz out of office. Chaos and the Revolution ensued. During the Revolution, contending forces convoked two constitutional conventions. The first, at Aguascalientes in 1914, was so dominated by Villistas, Zapatistas, and socialists that it proved unacceptable to middle class "Constitutionalists" and was followed by three years of anarchy and civil war. The second, held in Querétaro in 1917, drafted the constitution that has been Mexico's charter since the Revolution. Do Mexico's current circumstances warrant a new constitutional convention?

According to the Zapatistas, they do. Rejecting the peace accords in June 1994, the Zapatistas' *Segunda Declaración de la Selva Lacandona* stated that "the Carta Magna [i.e., Constitution] that governs us is no longer the will of the Mexican people . . . . [We need] new national law, a new Constitution, one that guarantees implementation of the popular will."[2] The statement called for a convention of delegates designated by "civilians" from *ejidos*, colonies, schools, and factories to meet in EZLN territory at an opportune time and place.

Other Mexicans have been making similar proposals. Amado Avendaño Figueroa, owner of San Cristóbal de las Casas's independent newspaper, *Tiempo*, served as the PRD candidate for governor of the state of Chiapas. In his platform he promised to form a transitional state government while convoking a convention drawn from "civil society" to write a new *Constitución Política de Chiapas*—in this case under the provisions of the existing 1917 Constitution that empowers citizens to change their form of government.[3]

Neither proposal clarifies just who belongs or does not belong to "civil society," but this imprecision did not deter a large group of independent peasant organizations and citizens from meeting in Tuxtla Gutiérrez in a self-proclaimed Chiapas State Democratic Convention on July 2 and 3, 1994, to endorse both proposals. On July 9, the Zapatistas and the leaders of the state convention issued a convocation for an August 6–9 National Democratic Convention, this time claiming a basis in the existing constitution. Several thousand people responded to the EZLN invitation. The convention was held before the elections, at the beginning of August in a place in the Selva Lacandona called "Aguascalientes"—in memory of the Revolution's first constitutional convention in 1914, signaling the intention to draft a more radical constitution than that on which Mexican government currently is based. Although many were supporters of PRD candidate Cuauhtémoc Cárdenas, the assembly refused to endorse any candidate and pledged to take to the streets in the event of a PRI "victory."[4]

Meanwhile, in San Cristóbal de las Casas, the reaction against supposed Zapatista sympathizers—individuals and groups (including the Church) who supported the peace negotiations—has crescendoed into death threats. Fear of an indigenous uprising is widespread among the ladino poor.

It has become clear that many indigenous and peasant groups have gained both the courage and the political consciousness to demand revindication for their grievances. Such groups say they have been awakened by the Zapatista uprising, and some of them have embraced the organizational structure adopted by the Zapatistas (ie., communal decision making, bottom-up management). In Zinacantán, a broad-based citizens' group formed a *Consejo Municipal* (municipal council) to govern the township with responsibility to what Zinacantecos are calling "the base" (i.e., "the masses"), after charging that the incumbent municipal president, Domingo Vázquez Jiménez, and his associates had misappropriated public works money and solidarity funds. Rumors spread that Vázquez held a private account in Oaxaca with deposits over US$270,000. The state legislature declined to depose Vázquez; Zinacantecos proceeded to take matters into their own hands by beating Vázquez and jailing him along with others accused of corruption.[5]

Prospects

What do Chiapas—and Mexico—have to look forward to in the wake of the Zapatista rebellion and the 1994 elections?

There is, of course, the very real possibility of further armed confrontation. Either the Zapatistas or the government could break the truce that has held since January 12, and hostilities could resume at any point. One cannot rule out the possibility that the military might renew its advance against the Zapatistas unilaterally, by way of a coup. The ensuing conflict would extend well beyond Chiapas.

It would be nice if Mexico could effect a transition to a new government and accommodation of the Zapatistas without incident. But even if that were to happen, the peace would not last unless policy makers were to take into account the underlying structural changes that have sharpened the agrarian crisis and reshaped peasant agricultural production.

The time has passed for considering the "peasant question" simply in terms of price guarantees for corn or redistribution of land for labor-intensive household-based production. While peasants do continue to produce for subsistence and survival, their livelihoods also range off the farm, not just in wage work, but in a wide array of activities that combine surprisingly modern and flexible enterprise with collective or cooperative endeavor.

Zinacantecos, for example, use cooperative trading arrangements in their wholesale and retail marketing of flowers. Rather than competing individually in the flower trade, groups of Zinacantecos band together to market flowers. Robert Alvarez and I (1994) found that Zinacanteco flower merchants who supply the markets of Tuxtla Gutiérrez work in groups of up to six or eight associates selling flowers at a given market stall. Members work together to bulk and ship goods they obtain from local producers, even though each purchases his produce separately. Every day, a different member of the group travels to Tuxtla Gutiérrez to sell. Members rotate the use of the market stall among their group, sharing the risk of fixed expenses as well as the opportunities for profit, leaving each member enough time for farming milpa or for other activities.

Most Chiapanecans do not realize that Zinacantecos travel as far as Mexico City to obtain flowers for southern markets, and that while Zinacantecos are investing in plastic greenhouses to produce flowers in the Chiapas highlands, they are also procuring as many as half of the flowers sold in central Chiapas from wholesale markets in central Mexico. One of my godsons belongs to one of six groups of Zinacantecos who pay a trucker to make a weekly round trip to Mexico City to purchase flowers. Each group sends one of its members, on a rotating basis, to buy flowers for his associates. For such trips to be profitable, the 8-ton truck must return from Mexico City fully loaded, hauling far more produce than any given group can afford alone. In effect, a large number of vendors are sharing the costs, risks, and profits available to those involved in national commercial circuits by banding together. Doing so allows them to capture some of the profit that would otherwise go to shippers and to realize economies of scale unavailable to individual vendors. Like many Zinacantecos, these flower vendors use at least part of their off-farm proceeds to pay for chemical inputs to intensify their farming.[6]

It is encouraging to me that peasant organizations in Chiapas have also been experimenting with alternatives to chemical-intensive agrarian technologies of the "green revolution." Many peasants *have* embraced the use of chemical fertilizers and labor-reducing herbicides that were heavily promoted by government agencies and advisors to many of the independent peasant organizations. But others have been encouraged by niche markets to draw upon centuries of experience with nonchemical multiple cropping to intensify organic production. For example, ISMAM, an organization of indigenous peoples from the Sierra Madre of Motozintla, Chiapas, is undertaking the production of organic coffee for markets in Canada, the United States, the Netherlands, Germany, and Switzerland. In Pantelhó, Indians have formed a cooperative with the assistance of a French agronomist to produce and market organic honey.[7] Environmentally sustainable production needs to be encouraged, and peasants should undertake more multicropping to protect themselves against fickle markets that expose producers to devastation when world prices of a given cash crop collapse.

Economists and planners need to recognize in such examples how diverse and flexible peasants' enterprises can be. In an epoch of global change that rewards those who tailor production to niches of economic opportunity, peasants are demonstrating they can do just that. Those who plan agrarian development need to recognize the potential of such peasant enterprise. They need to plan beyond agricultural extension in peasant communities to develop the infrastructures for transport, marketing, and commerce that help peasants diversify their livelihoods and invigorate the agrarian economy.

A recent study of NAFTA's impact on peasant corn producers argues that just such infrastructural support is needed to facilitate either the modernization of corn production to reach higher yields or the diversification into nontraditional fruits, vegetables, or field crops. Yet economic restructuring has removed the essential government services of credit, technical assistance, insurance, marketing, and agricultural advising precisely at the time when peasants need such services to diversify and modernize their production.[8]

I believe that Mexican economists also need to reconsider the relationship Mexico's agrarian economy has to the world economy.

A decent living in the countryside and the value of subsistence foods need to be factored into the equations that set the terms in which the country balances agrarian needs against those of urban-industrial producers and consumers. In addition, a modest devaluation of the peso could do much to help small producers of coffee and corn recuperate from recent market setbacks. Since the devaluation of Mexican currency after the debt crisis, Mexico has controlled its rate of exchange to reign in inflation. But some Mexican and North American economists argue that the peso now is overvalued by as much as 5 to 20 percent.[9] The artificially strong peso reduces the cost of imports encouraged by NAFTA, but it also creates a disadvantage for Mexican producers whose crops are destined for foreign markets or compete with imported foods. Those who claim that peasant corn is not competitive with imported corn have ignored the impact of Mexico's overvalued currency on domestic prices.

The Zapatistas have emphasized agrarian reform as central to their demands: work, land, housing, nutrition, health, education, independence, freedom, democracy, and justice. Other independent organizations in the region have emphasized marketing and credits as adjuncts to enhance peasant production on the farm. It is important to recognize that a variety of off-farm commercial enterprises can also play a role in agrarian development, and that peasants have the capacity to develop such enterprise to capture the profits that customarily have gone to others.

Planners also have something important to learn from existing peasant corporative associations and from the Zapatistas about accountability, namely that government agencies and public institutions must be accountable to the constituencies they serve—rather than vice versa.

Figure 7.1 **Organizational Chart, Unión de Ejidos "Profesor Otilio Montaño."**

In this regard, I am struck by the organization of the *Unión de Ejidos "Profesor Otilio Montaño,"* an *ejidal* union near Motozintla in the Pacific coastal range of Chiapas. Made up of sixteen member *ejidos* and six additional settlements, this union is dedicated to the organic production of coffee, apples, beans, corn, honey, and mushrooms for niche markets in Mexico and abroad. Its administrative organization places the union's general assembly *on top* and its administrators and officers on the bottom, symbolically inverting the hierarchies of power that are familiar to us for most corporations and governmental entities. It is notable that the Zapatistas describe themselves as similarly organized with popular assemblies governing the "Clandestine Committee of Indigenous Revolution," to which Sub-Comandante Marcos is in turn subordinate. Whether or not the Zapatistas or *ejidal* unions fully achieve the ideal that Marcos has described in terms of leaders who serve and who obey the will of the many, such commitment to accountability beckons powerfully to people who have experienced decades of disenfranchisement in which politicians, bureaucrats, and power holders treat the populace as beholden to them rather than vice versa.

A broader accountability is also called for on behalf of those who have been disadvantaged by the growing differentiation in the Mexican countryside. It is alarming to me that new alignments of wealth and power in peasant communities allow leaders to turn their backs on their poorest and weakest compatriots, among whom women and children have most to lose. But I am equally alarmed by the willingness of planners, in Mexico and in our own society, to shuck off responsibility for the impoverished for the sake of economic restructuring, especially when restructuring has actually swelled the ranks of the homeless, the unemployed, and those women and men who must work at multiple minimum-wage jobs with no benefits just to survive. In Mexico as in the United States, federal and state governments have sacrificed social safety nets in the name of austerity and free-market minimal governance. Mexico is now paying the costs of such benign (yet actually callous) neglect.

More generally, "modernizers" need to reconsider whether our societies can afford the impoverization of the masses that accompanies economic restructuring. Corporations pursue cheap labor and hefty profits on a global scale that escapes responsibility for conditions in any given nation. But concentrations of new wealth do not readily trickle down to the masses. In the final analysis, can modern economies and modern states afford societies in which so many people are losing their economic power as purchasers and consumers? The Zapatistas are forcing North Americans—citizens of Canada, the United States, and Mexico—to ponder this question.

Notes

Preface

1. Rosaldo (1989:68ff.)

Introduction

1. The survey was conducted by Lourdes Arizpe and her colleagues (Arizpe, Paz, and Velázquez, 1993).
2. From *Declaración de la Selva Lacandona* emitted by the *Comandancia General del EZLN* from the Selva Lacandona, Chiapas, Mexico on December 31, 1993.
3. e.g., Arvide (1994); Guillén (1994); Méndez and Cano (1994); Romero (1994).
4. Indigenous people generally speak one of the native American languages as their first tongue, though many also learn some Spanish. Many indigenous people identify themselves as members of ethnic communities that were classified as "Indian" rather than "Spanish" or *mestizo* (mixed race) under the period of colonial rule. There are also indigenous people who lack such links to specific communities because they have been diasporic throughout history. Indigenous people often experience discrimination and subordination at the hands of nonindigenous Mexicans.
5. See Williams (1986) on Central American radical movements as responding to peasants' displacement into marginal lands by developing commercial agriculture and ranching oriented to exports.

Chapter 1 - Chiapas and Mexico

1. *Tiempo,* February 4, 1992, p. 2.
2. Benjamin (1989).
3. See Pick (1989) for a convenient compilation of census and statistical data for Mexico in 1980. I use the 1980 data to illustrate Chiapas's situation relative to other parts of Mexico because some of the pertinent 1990 data has not yet been published by the Mexican government.
4. The statistical maps in this book use Mexican population and agrarian census data for townships in Chiapas and in some instances for townships in Tabasco and adjacent areas of the states of Oaxaca and Veracruz.
5. Nations (1994).
6. Ruz (1985).
7. Nations (1994); de Vos (1980, 1988).
8. MacLeod (1973); Wasserstrom (1983).
9. Helms (1975).
10. See also Ruz (1992) for characterization of colonial-era ranches in eastern Chiapas.
11. Gosner (1992); Viqueira (1993).
12. Bricker (1981:60).
13. Chiapas continued to have significant linkages to Guatemala after Independence. See Fábregas, et. al., (1985) for one of a series of new

studies of Mexico's *"frontera sur"* in relation to linkages of economy, migration, politics, and culture.

14. See Wolf and Hansen (1972) for an insightful discussion of the export enclaves and their impact in Latin America.

15. de Vos (1988).

16. These coffee plantations, which still produce as much as 30 percent of Mexico's coffee exports, in turn stimulated the development of Chiapas's central Grijalva River valley as a breadbasket for the Soconusco, while drawing Indians from the central highlands to work as laborers. (Helbig 1964; Taller Tzotzil 1990.) The Soconusco area coffee plantations were essentially similar to those in Guatemala documented by the photographer Eadweard Muybridge near the turn of the century; see Burns (1986).

17. Jan Rus (1983, 1989).

18. Wasserstrom (1983).

19. Jan Rus (1994:268-272); Taller Tzotzil (1988).

20. Benjamin (1989:55ff.).

21. Wolf (1969) provides a useful overview of the different revolutionary groups, their goals, and their relationships to the regionally different histories of development in Mexico.

22. Merryman (1969).

23. In light of the current uprising, it is also worth noting that the 1917 Constitution embodied no special provisions for Indians. Mexican and many other Latin American thinkers of the time conceived of the *mestizo* as the quintessential national citizen. Mexico's philosopher/educator José Vasconcelos argued that the *mestizo* combined the best features of the Iberian and the Indian into a superior race, Vasconcelos's *La Raza Cósmica* (1948). Arguing that Indians should be educated and assimilated, Vasconcelos launched an ambitious rural literacy crusade when he became Minister of Education in the 1920s. Other thinkers, notably Manuel Gamio in *Forjando Patria* (*Forging a Nation*), argued that Mexico's many distinct indigenous heritages were mini-nationalities whose cultural assets should be acknowledged and brought, along with Indians, into the post-revolutionary national project. Diego de Rivera and other public works muralists of the 1920s, gave expression to this willingness to embrace the Indian as a contributor of culture to Mexican national society—as did the federal Indianist programs of later decades.

24. Benjamin (1989:119ff); Jan Rus (n.d.).

25. García de León (1991); Benjamin (1989:123ff).

26. García de León (1985); Burguete, in a talk she gave at Stanford in spring 1994; Nigh (1994). García de León, writing about the control that Chiapas oligarchs have held virtually until the present day, sees the reactionary Mapaches as merely part of a continuous succession of power holders that have governed Chiapas in the interest of the land-holding families, including that of recent ex-governor Absalón Castellanos Domínguez, whom the EZLN kidnapped on January 1, 1994.

27. Spenser (1988).

28. See Wilkie (1970) for an overview of the Mexican agrarian reform from the Revolution through the middle of the century.
29. See Sanderson (1986:241-250) for an overview of Mexican agrarian policy in the post-war period.
30. Collier (1975, 1987a); Jan Rus (1976:23-26); Wasserstrom (1983:162-167). Most of the land given over to peasants was marginal, yet suitable for peasant *milpa* cultivation. In the Soconusco, peasants received coffee-producing lands in agrarian reform; see Ascencio (1994) for a discussion of the relations between peasant coffee production in the Soconusco and its relation to production on larger estates.
31. Warman (1980) was one of the first in calling attention to the intensification of peasant production spurred by Mexican fiscal policies.
32. Aguirre Beltrán (1955); de la Fuente (1953). See Pineda (1993) for an interesting analysis of how INI bilingual schoolteachers and promoters gained positions of power in their communities as a result of their work.

Chapter 2 - Eastern Chiapas: Land

1. At conquest, the inhabitants of this region were known as the Lacandón. All of the original Lacandón died out or were removed in slaving expeditions. Later, the region was repopulated by indigenous refugees from other areas. Many have mistakenly taken them to be descendants of the Lacandón of conquest times. For the story of the original Lacandón, see de Vos (1980).
2. Cancian and Brown (1994).
3. Iribarren (1987:16).
4. See Parra (1989, 1993) on the dilemmas of highland Chiapas production on what are for many people tiny plots of land.
5. Earle (1994); Pohlenz (1985:70).
6. See Ascencio and Lleyva's Table 4 (1992:207-208); see also Arizpe, et. al., (1993:81) for data on colonists from other states in eastern Chiapas.
7. Ascencio and Leyva (1992:181, fn. 9).
8. Nations (1984:38); See Nigh and Nations (1980) on the multicropping potentials of tropical forest cultivation.
9. See Garza, Paz, Ruiz and Calvo (1993) for indigenous women's accounts of the settling of this community.
10. Pohlenz (1985).
11. Ascencio and Leyva (1992:194).
12. Leyva and Ascencio (1993); see also Earle (1994) for a discussion of enterprises taken up in the colony of Nuevo Chamula.
13. Cornelius (1992) gives a concise yet thorough summary of the changes made in Article 27 and the Agrarian Code.
14. Gossen (1994:20).
15. *Tiempo*, January 20, 1994, p. 3.
16. *New York Times*, February 27, 1994, p. 6.
17. Reyes Ramos (1992:101-2).
18. In Las Margaritas and Ocosingo, claims were resolved in 5.6 years and 5.79 years respectively, on average, as compared to 7.36 years for Chiapas as a whole, according to Reyes Ramos (1992:150-151).

19. Reyes Ramos (1992:93-95).
20. Benjamin (1989:232).
21. Pohlenz (1985:72).
22. The Montes Azul bioreserve was granted 330,312 hectares, according to Nations (1984:39).
23. The relocation centers were Palestina (later renamed Velasco Suárez) for the Tzeltal-speaking colonists, Corozal (later renamed Echeverría) for the Chol speakers, and Lacanjá Chan Sayab, Mensabak, and Najá for the 400 Lacandón Indians (Nations 1994:32).
24. Iribarren (1988:30).
25. The most important independent organizations were the Union of Unions (UU), the Emiliano Zapata Peasant Organization (OCEZ), and the Independent Confederation of Agricultural Workers and Peasants (CIOAC). The PRA largely bypassed their peasant affiliates (Reyes Ramos 1992:113-118).

Chapter 3 - Eastern Chiapas: The Building of Social Movements

1. e.g., *Tiempo*, January 5, 1994, p. 5.
2. *Proceso*, 7 June 1993, pp. 18-21; *La Jornada*, 2 August 1993, pp. 1 and 10; *Proceso*, 13 September 1993, pp.12-13, 15.
3. Fox 1994a; Harvey 1994.
4. *New York Times*, February 21, 1994, p. A7.
5. See Bastian (1983, 1990) on the history of Protestantism in Mexico and Latin America; see Hernández Castillo 1993 for a review of the literature on Protestantism in Chiapas.
6. Gossen (1989, 1994).
7. Comisión Nacional de Derechos Humanos (1992).
8. The debates over the conflict between exiles and "traditionalists" take place in the context of a larger debate as to whether and how to grant autonomy and cultural rights to indigenous communities. See Díaz Polanco (1991, 1992) for a discussion of the Salinas government's proposed revisions of Article 4 of the Constitution to grant indigenous autonomy. See also a special issue of *Cuadernos de la Gaceta* (Vol. 1, No. 1, 1993) concerning "Derechos de los pueblos indígenas."
9. Giménez Montiel (1988).
10. Hernández Castillo (1989).
11. Cancian (1965).
12. Hernández Castillo (1994).
13. *Tiempo*, February 1, 1994, p. 3.
14. *Tiempo*, February 6, 1994, p. 4.
15. Morales Bermúdez (1992:314-348, *passim.*)
16. I myself have witnessed the corrupt sale of quack medicines by a public health nurse in a rural community in Chiapas who also charged patients the equivalent of a rural dayworker's wage for doses of medicines that health authorities had provided her for free distribution.
17. *Tiempo*, March 5, 6, 1994, *passim*.
18. Morales Bermúdez (1992:259-263). See also Leyva's (1994) discussion

of the galvanizing effect of Catholic evangelizing on the peasant organizing in the Cañadas region of Las Margaritas.

19. *Tiempo*, February 5, 1944, p. 5.
20. *Tiempo*, January 12, 1994, p. 3.
21. *Tiempo*, January 19, 1994, p. 3.
22. e.g., Roger Bartra (1974, 1975, 1978, 1982). See Hewitt de Alcántara (1984) for an incisive analysis of the Mexican debate on the peasantry, and my discussion of the debate with reference to analysis of highland Chiapas (George Collier, 1992).
23. e.g., Armando Bartra (1979); note that Roger Bartra and Armando Bartra hold opposing positions with regard to the peasantry.
24. Flores, Paré, and Sarmiento (1988:66-80).
25. Hernández Navarro (1994).
26. Armando Bartra (1985); Encinas and Rascón (1983:203ff); Flores, Paré, and Sarmiento (1988:80-89); Harvey (1988); Taller de Análisis de las Cuestiones Agrarias (1988); Varese (1992).
27. Paré (1988).
28. Alvarez (1988); Brown (1993:183-196); Marion (1984); Pérez Castro (1989); Sánchez and Ovalle (1986); Taller de Análisis de las Cuestiones Agrarias (1988), Toledo Tello (n.d.).
29. Oswald, Rodríguez, and Flores (1986)
30. *Proceso*, 13 September 1993, pp.12-13.
31. *Proceso*, 13 September 1993, p. 15.
32. Harvey (1994); Taller de Análisis de las Cuestiones Agrarias (1988:57-58).
33. Harvey (1994); Leyva (1994); Taller de Análisis de las Cuestiones Agrarias (1988).
34. Unión Tierra Tzotzil (1990); Jan Rus, personal communication.
35. Marcos to CEOIC, the Chiapas State Indigenous Peasant Council, a state-level federation of peasant and indigenous organizations, *Tiempo*, February 8, 1994, p. 3.
36. *Tiempo*, May 27, 1994, p. 1.
37. Taller de Análisis de las Cuestiones Agrarias (1988:22); Brown (1993:157); Encinas and Rascón (1984:32); Burguete (1987:xvi).
38. Taller de Análisis de las Cuestiones Agrarias (1988:2).
39. Americas Watch (1990); Minnesota Advocates for Human Rights (1993).
40. *Tiempo*, March 4, 1994, p. 5.
41. *Resumen Informativo* 25:26. This monthly was published by the Centro de Información y Análisis de Chiapas (CIACH), San Cristóbal de las Casas, until just before the EZLN uprising. A partial run is available in the Stanford University Libraries.
42. *Tiempo*, February 5, 1994, p. 6 and February 6, 1994, p. 3.
43. EZLN leaders to journalists, *Tiempo*, February 5, 1994, p. 6.
44. Marcos, to *Tiempo*, January 18, 1994, p. 4.
45. Gordillo (1992).
46. Marion (1994:20).
47. *El Sureste*, March 19, 1994, p. 1.

48. *Tiempo,* February 9, 1994, p. 2.
49. *Tiempo,* February 9, 1994, p. 2; February 10, 1994, p. 3.
50. *Proceso,* September 13, 1993, pp. 13, 15.
51. *Tiempo,* February 6, 1994, p. 2.
52. *Tiempo,* February 11, 1994, p. 3 (through a printer's error, this issue is dated February 10).
53. *Tiempo,* February 11, 1994, p. 3.
54. *Tiempo,* February 11, 1994, pp. 3-4.
55. *Tiempo,* February 6, 1994, p. 3.
56. *Tiempo,* February 6, 1994, p. 3.
57. *Tiempo,* February 6, 1994, p. 3.

Chapter 4 - Oil and the Crisis in Mexican Agriculture

1. Cancian (1989:165).
2. Taller Tzotzil (1988, 1990).
3. See Pietri and Stern (1985) on the impact of oil development on Mexico's southeast; Karl (n.d.) compares Mexican oil development to that of other oil exporting countries after OPEC; Hirschman (1981) also discusses the impact of Mexican oil-led development. This discussion draws upon Collier, Mountjoy and Nigh (1994).
4. See Corden (1984) for a review and overview of development economists' concept of "Dutch disease." Scherr (1985) discusses the mixed impact of the "oil syndrome" on the agriculture of Tabasco.
5. Sanderson (1986:241); Spalding (1984).
6. See Armando Bartra (1979); Esteva (1983); and Barkin and Suárez (1985), or Barkin (1987).
7. Based on Collier, Mountjoy, and Nigh (1994) Figure 2, and data from Karl (n.d.).
8. Hewitt de Alcántara (1992), for example, assembled analyses of Mexican maize pricing policy to help assess what the impact on peasants would be of removing price guarantees for maize.
9. See George Collier (1989, 1990, 1994a); Collier and Mountjoy (1988). Burbach (1994) has drawn on this work in his interpretation of the Zapatista rebellion. For general background on Zinacantán, see Vogt (1969) and Cancian (1965, 1972, 1989, 1992).
10. Cancian (1992); George Collier (1990).
11. George Collier (1990); Flood (1994).
12. Dewey (1981).
13. Scherr (1985).
14. George Collier and Mountjoy (1988).
15. Grindle (1988) finds similar diversification of livelihoods in other parts of Mexico.
16. Alvarez and Collier (1994) discuss the Zinacanteco trucking and flower enterprises and compare them to trucking and produce businesses in northern Mexico. Nigh (1992) discusses the small business collectives or "corporative associations" that Mexican peasants are developing in many arenas of production and marketing.

17. Rosenbaum (1993:121); Diane Rus (1990); Jan Rus (personal communication).
18. Loyola (1988).
19. *San Francisco Chronicle*, June 13, 1994, p. A6.
20. Pohlenz (1985).
21. Pohlenz (1985).
22. Harvey (1994:9-11) has a particularly useful summary of the deterioration in pricing of various crops critical to peasant market-oriented production.

Chapter 5 - The Toll of Restructuring on Lives and Communities

1. Nash (1994) reviews this problem in global perspective and notes the parallels among the plights of urban and rural poor in the context of restructuring on a global scale.
2. Rosenbaum (1993). Chamula has greater extremes of poverty and wealth than most indigenous communities in Chiapas, and it has received far more governmental attention.
3. Diane Rus (1988, 1990).
4. See Cancian (1965, 1972); G. Collier (1975) on Zinacanteco farming strategies and technology.
5. Diane Rus, 1988. See George Collier (1989, 1990) for the Zinacanteco case.
6. Diane Rus (1988); see also Eber and Rosenbaum (1993) and Flood (1994) on women's weaving as a response to economic crisis in highland Chiapas, and Nash (1993) on similar responses in other parts of the world.
7. Jan Rus (1994).
8. Cancian's (1965) study of the Zinacanteco "cargo" system of civil and religious posts showed how Zinacantecos converted their wealth into prestige and community-wide reputation.
9. Nash and Sullivan (1992).
10. The revised Article 27 and Agrarian Code are conveniently available in Gaceta de Solidaridad (1992) and have been summarized and assessed in Cornelius (1992) and DeWalt and Rees (1994). See Gaceta de Solidaridad (1992) and Gordillo (1992) on positive changes intended by reformulation of Article 27 and the Agrarian Code. See also my assessment of the probable impact of the changes on peasant tenure in highland Chiapas (George Collier, 1994c).

Chapter 6 - Exclusion: The New Politics

1. The first three sections of this chapter are based on G. Collier (1994b) by permission of Kluwer Academic Publishers.
2. See my article on Zinacanteco politics (George Collier 1994b) for a more extended discussion of the new politics of exclusion.
3. The revisions to the penal code appear in *Periódico Oficial* [Tuxtla Gutiérrez, Chiapas] 99(1):31-36 [1988].
4. Minnesota Advocates for Human Rights (1993:48, ix).

5. See Jane Collier (1973) on Zinacanteco customary law and its relation to Mexican national law.
6. Cancian (1992:46-47, 127-150).
7. *Tiempo*, April 8, 1989, p. 1.
8. See Jane Collier (1977, 1979) for a comparison of Zinacantán and San Felipe in terms of different styles of litigation, and for a discussion of the changes taking place in Zinacanteco litigation.
9. For expulsions in 1989 from Oxchuc, see *Tiempo*, May 10, 1989; for Mitontic, *Tiempo* June 29, June 30, and July 1, 1989; for Amatenango del Valle, *Tiempo*, August 8, 1989; for Chenalhó, *Tiempo*, November 7, November 9, November 11, and November 14, 1989. See Morquecho (1992) for an overview of the independent organizing that brought many of the exiled groups together in the Indigenous Organization of Highland Chiapas (ORIACH).
10. e.g., Cornelius, Gentleman, and Smith (1989).
11. Russell (1994:66-69, 143-145).
12. Dresser (1991:6-7); Lustig (1994:88).
13. With emphasis as translated in Cornelius, Craig, and Fox (1994:7).
14. García and Pontigo (1993); Hernández Navarro and Célis (1994); Villafuerte (1993).
15. Hernández Navarro and Célis (1994:229).
16. Fox (1994b).
17. *La Jornada*, March 21, 1992, p. 13.
18. Harvey (1994:20).
19. *Tiempo*, February 25, 1994, p. 1.
20. e.g., Burguete (1987).

Chapter 7 - Transitions and Prospects

1. *Proceso*, June 20, 1994, p.12.
2. p. 6 of supplement to June 14, 1994 issue of *Tiempo*.
3. *Tiempo*, June 16, 1994, pp. 2-3.
4. *Tiempo*, July 5, 1994, p. 2; *La Jornada*, July 10, 1994, p. 12. *San Francisco Chronicle*, August 11, 1994, p. 1.
5. *Proceso*, July 18, 1994, p. 34.
6. See Collier, Mountjoy and Nigh (1994) for an analysis of the impact of Zinacanteco off-farm enterprize on the use of purchased inputs in farming.
7. See Victor Toledo (1994) on the potentials of peasant multicropping micro-enterprize. See Cortina (1993) and ISMAM (1990) on organic coffee production and organizations in the Soconusco. See Brown (1993:237) on the Pantelhó honey cooperative.
8. See de Janvry, Sadoulet, and Gordillo (1994:11) on the needs of infrastructure to facilitate restructuring in peasant production.
9. On overvaluation of the peso, see interview with Massachusetts Institute of Technology economist Paul Krugman in *El Financiero*, June 19, 1994, p. 4; and discussion, *El Financiero*, June 22, 1994, p. 5.

References

Aguirre Beltrán, Gonzalo
1955　A Theory of Regional Integration: The Coordinating Centers. *América Indígena* 15(1):29-42.

Alvarez, Fernando
1988　Peasant Movements in Chiapas. *Bulletin of Latin American Research* 7:277-298.

Alvarez, Robert, and George A. Collier
1994　The Long Haul in Mexican Trucking: Traversing the Borderlands of the North and the South. *American Ethnologist* 21(3):606-627.

Americas Watch
1990　*Human Rights in Mexico: A Policy of Impunity.* An Americas Watch Report. New York: Human Rights Watch.

Arizpe, Lourdes, Fernanda Paz, and Margarita Velázquez
1993　*Cultura y Cambio Global: Percepciones Sociales sobre la Deforestación en la Selva Lacandona.* México, D.F.: UNAM - Centro Regional de Investigaciones Multidisciplinarias/Grupo Editorial Miguel Angel Porrúa, S.A.

Arvide, Isabel
1994　*Crónica de una Guerra Anunciada.* México, D.F.: Grupo Editorial Siete, S.A.

Ascencio Franco, Gabriel
1994　Integración finca-ejido en la cafeticultura del Soconusco. Pp. 66-97 in *El café en la frontera sur,* ed. by Daniel Villafuerte Solís. Tuxtla Gutiérrez: Instituto Chiapaneco de Cultura.

Ascencio Franco, Gabriel and Xóchitl Leyva Solano
1992　Los municipios de la Selva Chiapaneca, Colonización y dinámica agropecuaria. *Anuario 1991, Instituto Chiapaneco de Cultura,* pp. 176-241.

Barkin, David
1987　The End to Food Self-Sufficiency in Mexico. *Latin American Perspectives* 14(3):271-297.

Barkin, David, and Blanca Suárez
1985　*El fin de la autosuficiencia alimentaria.* México, D.F.: Centro de Ecodesarrollo/Ediciones Océano, S.A.

Bartra, Armando
1979　*La explotación del trabajo campesino por el capital.* México D.F.: Editorial Macehual.

1985　*Los herederos de Zapata: Movimientos campesinos posrevolucionarios en México.* México, D.F.: Ediciones Era.

Bartra, Roger
1974　*Estructura agraria y clases sociales en México.* México D.F.: Editorial Era.

1975　Peasants and Political Power in Mexico: A Theoretical Approach. *Latin American Perspectives* 2(2).

1978　*El poder despótico burgués.* México D.F.: Editorial Era.

1982　Capitalism and the Peasantry in Mexico. *Latin American Perspectives* 9(1).

Bastian, Jean-Pierre
1983　*Protestantismo y Sociedad en México.* México, D.F.: Casa Unida de Publicaciones, S.A. (CUPSA).

1990   *Historia del Protestantismo en América Latina.* México, D.F.: Centro de Comunicación Cultural CUPSA, A.C.

Benjamin, Thomas
1989   *A Rich Land, A Poor People: Politics and Society in Modern Chiapas.* Albuquerque: University of New Mexico Press.

Bricker, Victoria Reifler
1981   *The Indian Christ, the Indian King: The Historical Substrate of Maya Myth and Ritual.* Austin: University of Texas Press.

Brown, Pete
1993   *The Creation of Community: Class and Ethnic Struggle in Pantelho, Chiapas, Mexico.* Ph.D. Dissertation, Division of Social Science, University of California, Irvine.

Burbach, Roger
1994   Roots of the Postmodern Rebellion in Chiapas. *New Left Review* 205:113-124.

Burguete Cal y Mayor, Araceli
1987   *Chiapas: Cronología de un etnocidio reciente. (Represión política a los indios 1974-1987).* Unpublished manuscript, Academia Mexicana de Derechos Humanos, A.C., 1987.

Burns, E. Bradford
1986   *Eadweard Muybridge in Guatemala, 1875: The Photographer as Social Recorder.* Berkeley: University of California Press.

Cancian, Frank
1965   *Economics and Prestige in a Maya Community.* Stanford, CA: Stanford University Press.
1972   *Change and Uncertainty in a Peasant Economy: The Maya Corn Farmers of Zinacantan.* Stanford, CA: Stanford University Press.
1989   Economic behavior in peasant communities. Pages 127-170 in *Economic Anthropology*, Stuart Plattner, ed. Stanford, CA: Stanford University Press.
1992   *The Decline of Community in Zinacantan: Economy, Public Life, and Social Stratification, 1960-1987.* Stanford, CA: Stanford University Press.

Cancian, Frank and Peter Brown
1994   Who is Rebelling in Chiapas? *Cultural Survival Quarterly* 18(1):22-25.

Castellanos, Rosario
1992   *The Nine Guardians.* Columbia, LA. and London: Readers International, Inc. First published in Spanish as *Balún Canán* in 1957 by the Fondo de Cultura Económica, México, D.F.

Collier, George A.
1975   *Fields of the Tzotzil: The Ecological Bases of Tradition in Highland Chiapas.* Austin: University of Texas Press.
1987a   Peasant Politics and the Mexican State: Indigenous Compliance in Highland Chiapas. *Mexican Studies/Estudios Mexicanos*, 3:71-98.
1987b   *Socialists of Rural Andalusia: Unacknowledged Revolutionaries of the Second Republic.* Stanford, CA: Stanford University Press.
1989   Changing Inequality in Zinacantan: The Generations of 1918 and 1942. Pp. 111-124 in Victoria R. Bricker and Gary H. Gossen, eds. *Ethnographic Encounters in Southern Mesoamerica: Essays in Honor of Evon Zartman Vogt,*

Jr. Studies on Culture and Society, Volume 3, Institute for Mesoamerican Studies, The University at Albany, State University of New York.

1990 *Seeking Food and Seeking Money: Changing Productive Relations in a Highland Mexican Community.* Discussion Paper 10, United Nations Research Institute for Social Development, Geneva.

1992 Los Zinacantecos en su mundo contemporáneo. Pp. 189-215 in *Antropología Mesoamericana: Homenaje a Alfonso Villa Rojas*, ed. by Victor Manuel Esponda, Sophia Pincemin, and Mauricio Rosas. Tuxtla Gutiérrez: Instituto Chiapaneco de Cultura.

1994a Roots of the Rebellion in Chiapas. *Cultural Survival Quarterly* 18(1):14-18.

1994b The New Politics of Exclusion: Antecedents to the Rebellion in Mexico. *Dialectical Anthropology* 19(1):1-44.

1994c Reforms of Mexico's agrarian code: impacts on the peasantry. *Research in Economic Anthropology* 15:105-127.

1994d The Rebellion in Chiapas and the Legacy of Energy Development. *Mexican Studies/Estudios Mexicanos* 10(2):371-382.

Collier, George A. and Daniel C. Mountjoy

1988 *Adaptándose a la crisis de los Ochenta: Cambios socio-económicos en Apás, Zinacantán.* Documento 035-II/88. San Cristóbal de las Casas: Instituto de Asesoría Antropológica para la Region Maya, A.C.,

Collier, George A., Daniel Mountjoy, and Ronald B. Nigh

1994 Peasant Agriculture and Global Change: A Maya Response to Energy Development in Southeastern Mexico. *BioScience* 44:398-407.

Collier, Jane F.

1973 *Law and Social Change in Zinacantan.* Stanford: Stanford University Press.

1977 Political Leadership and Legal Change in Zinacantan. *Law and Society Review* 11(1):131-163.

1979 Stratification and Dispute Handling in Two Highland Chiapas Communities. *American Ethnologist* 6:305-327.

Comisión Nacional de Derechos Humanos

1992 *Informe sobre el problema de las expulsiones en las comunidades indígenas de los altos de Chiapas y los derechos humanos.* México, D.F.: CNDH.

Corden, Werner Max

1984 Booming sector and Dutch disease economics: Survey and consolidation. *Oxford Economic Papers* 36: 359-380.

Cornelius, Wayne A.

1992 The Politics and Economics of Reforming the *Ejido* Sector in Mexico: An Overview and Research Agenda. *LASA Forum* 23(3):3-10.

Cornelius, Wayne A., Ann L. Craig, and Jonathan Fox

1994 *Transforming State-Society Relations in Mexico: The National Solidarity Strategy.* La Jolla: Center for U.S.-Mexican Studies, University of California, San Diego.

Cornelius, Wayne A., Judith Gentleman, and Peter H. Smith, eds.

1989 *Mexico's Alternative Political Futures.* La Jolla: University of California, San Diego.

Cortina Villar, Sergio

1993 Sistemas de cultivo de café en el Soconusco. Pp. 52-65 in *El café en la frontera sur: La producción y los productores del Soconusco, Chiapas*, ed. by Daniel Villafuerte Solís. Tuxtla Gutiérrez: Instituto Chiapaneco de Cultura.

Dewalt, Billie R. and Martha W. Rees
1994   *The End of the Agrarian Reform in Mexico: Past Lessons, Future Prospects.* Transformation of Rural Mexico Series, No. 3. La Jolla: Center for U.S.-Mexican Studies, University of California, San Diego.

Dewey, K. G.
1981   Nutritional consequences of the transformation from subsistence to commercial agriculture in Tabasco, Mexico. *Human Ecology* 9: 151-187.

Díaz Polanco, Héctor
1991   *Autonomía regional: La autodeterminación de los pueblos indios.* México, D.F.: Siglo Veintiuno Editores.
1992   Derecho Nacional y derecho indígena: (Reflexiones en torno a la ley reglamentaria del artículo 4o. constitucional). [Working paper]. México, D.F., 1992.

Dresser, Denise
1991   *Neopopulist Solutions to Neoliberal Problems.* Current Issue Brief No. 3, Center for U.S.-Mexican Studies. La Jolla: University of California, San Diego.

Earle, Duncan
1994   Indigenous Identity at the Margin: Zapatismo and Nationalism. *Cultural Survival Quarterly* 18(1):26-29.

Eber, Christine, and Brenda Rosenbaum
1993   "That We May Serve beneath Your Hands and Feet": Women Weavers in Highland Chiapas, Mexico. Pp. 155-182 in *Impact of Global Exchange on Middle American Artisans.* June Nash, ed. Albany: SUNY Press.

Encinas R., Alejandro and Fernando Rascón F.
1983   *Reporte y Cronología del Movimiento Campesino e Indígena,* No. 3-4, Julio-Diciembre 1982. México, D.F.: Universidad Autónoma Chapingo.

Esteva, Gustavo
1983   *The Struggle for Rural Mexico.* South Hadley, Massachusetts: Bergin & Garvey Publishers, Inc.

Fábregas Puig, Andrés, Juan Pohlenz, Mariano Baez, and Gabriel Macías
1985   *La formación histórica de la frontera sur.* Cuadernos de La Casa Chata 124. México, D.F.: Centro de Investigaciones y Estudios Superiores en Antropología Social.

Flood, Merielle
1994   Changing patterns of interdependence: the effects of increasing monetization on gender relations in Zinacantan, Mexico. *Research in Economic Anthropology* 15:145-173.

Flores Lúa, Graciela, Luisa Paré, and Sergio Sarmiento Silva
1988   *Las voces del campo: Movimiento campesino y política agraria, 1976-1984.* México, D.F.: Siglo Veintiuno Editores.

Fox, Jonathan
1994a The Roots of Chiapas. *Boston Review* 19(2):24-27.
1994b Targeting the Poorest: The Role of the National Indigenous Institute in

Mexico's Solidarity Program. Pp. 179-216 in *Transforming State-Society Relations in Mexico: The National Solidarity Strategy*, ed. by Wayne A. Cornelius, Ann L. Craig, and Jonathan Fox. La Jolla: Center for U.S.-Mexican Studies, University of California, San Diego.

Frank, André Gunder
1967 *Capitalism and Underdevelopment in Latin America*. New York: Monthly Review Press.

de la Fuente, Julio
1953 El Centro Coordinador Tzeltal-Tzotzil: Una realización del México de hoy. *América Indígena* 13(1):55-64.

Gaceta de Solidaridad
1992 *Nueva legislación agraria: Articulo 27 constitucional, Ley Agraria, Ley Orgánica de los Tribunales Agrarios*. México, D.F.: Gaceta de Solidaridad.

Gamio, Manuel
1960 *Forjando patria*. México, D.F.: Editorial Porrúa.

García Aguilar, María del Carmen, and José Luis Pontigo Sánchez
1993 La política cafetalera y sus efectos en las organizaciones de productores del sector social del Soconusco. Pp. 121-135 in *El café en la frontera sur: La producción y los productores del Soconusco, Chiapas*, ed. by Daniel Villafuerte Solís. Tuxtla Gutiérrez: Instituto Chiapaneco de Cultura.

Garza Caligaris, Anna María, María Fernanda Paz Salinas, Juana María Ruiz Ortiz, and Angelino Calvo Sánchez
1993 *Sk'op Antzetik: Una historia de mujeres en la selva de Chiapas*. Tuxtla Gutiérrez, Chiapas: Universidad Autónoma de Chiapas.

García de León, Antonio
1985 *Resistencia y utopía: Memorial de agravios y crónica de revueltas y profecías acaecidas en la provincia de Chiapas durante los últimos quinientos años de su historia*. 2 vols. México, D.F.: Ediciones Era.
1991 *Ejército de ciegos: Testimonios de la guerra chiapaneca entre Carrancistas y rebeldes, 1914-1920*. México, D.F.: Ediciones Toledo.

Giménez Montiel, Gilberto
1988 *Sectas Religiosas en el Sureste: Aspectos Sociográficos y Estadísticos*. Cuadernos de La Casa Chata 161. México, D.F.: Centro de Investigaciones y Estudios Superiores en Antropología Social.

Gordillo de Anda, Gustavo
1992 *Más allá de Zapata: Por una reforma campesina*. México, D.F.: Cal y Arena.

Gosner, Kevin
1992 *Soldiers of the Virgin: The Moral Economy of a Colonial Maya Rebellion*. Tucson: University of Arizona Press.

Gossen, Gary H.
1989 Life, Death, and Apotheosis of a Chamula Protestant Leader. Pp. 217-229 in *Ethnographic Encounters in Southern Mesoamerica: Essays in Honor of Evon Zartman Vogt, Jr.*, Victoria R. Bricker and Gary H. Gossen, eds., Albany: Institute of Mesoamerican Studies, SUNY.
1994 Comments on the Zapatista Movement. *Cultural Survival Quarterly* 18(1):19-21.

Grindle, Merilee Serrill
1988   *Searching for Rural Development: Labor Migration and Employment in Mexico.* Cornell University Press: Ithaca, NY.

Guillén Trujillo, Julio Cesar
1994   *¿La guerra o la paz?* Tuxtla Gutiérrez: Editorial Diálogo.

Harvey, Neil
1988   Personal Networks and Strategic Choices in the Formation of an Independent Peasant Organization: The OCEZ of Chiapas, Mexico. *Bulletin of Latin American Research* 7:299-312.

1994   *Rebellion in Chiapas: Rural Reforms, Campesino Radicalism, and the Limits to Salinismo.* Transformation of Rural Mexico Series, No. 5. La Jolla, CA.: Center for U.S.-Mexican Studies, University of California at San Diego.

Helbig, Carlos
1964   *El Soconusco y su zona cafetalera en Chiapas.* Tuxtla Gutiérrez: Instituto de Ciencias y Artes de Chiapas.

Helms, Mary
1975   *Middle America: A Culture History of Heartland and Frontiers.* Englewood Cliffs, N.J.: Prentice Hall.

Hernández Castillo, Rosalva Aída
1989   Del Tzolkin a la Atalaya: Los cambios en la religiosidad en una comunidad Chuj-K'anhobal de Chiapas. Pp. 123-224 in *Religión y Sociedad en el Sureste de México,* Vol. 2, ed. by Andrés Fábregas, et. al. Cuadernos de La Casa Chata 162. México, D.F.: Centro de Investigaciones y Estudios Superiores en Antropología Social.

1993   Entre la victimización y la resistencia étnica: revisión crítica de la bibliografía sobre protestantismo en Chiapas. *Anuario 1992, Instituto Chiapaneco de Cultura*: 165-186.

1994   La "fuerza extraña" es mujer. *Ojarasca* 30:36-37.

Hernández Navarro, Luis
1994   The Chiapas Uprising. Pp. 44-56 in *Rebellion in Chiapas,* ed. by Neil Harvey. Transformation of Rural Mexico Series, No. 5. La Jolla, CA.: Center for U.S.-Mexican Studies, University of California at San Diego.

Hernández Navarro, Luis, and Fernando Célis Callejas
1994   Solidarity and the New Campesino Movements: The Case of Coffee Production. Pp. 217-231 in *Transforming State-Society Relations in Mexico: The National Solidarity Strategy,* ed. by Wayne A. Cornelius, Ann L. Craig, and Jonathan Fox. La Jolla: Center for U.S.-Mexican Studies, University of California, San Diego.

Hewitt de Alcántara, Cynthia
1984   *Anthropological Perspectives on Rural Mexico.* London: Routledge & Kegan Paul.

1992   *Reestructuración económica y subsistencia rural: El maíz y la crisis de los ochenta.* Edited by Cynthia Hewitt de Alcántara. México, D.F.: El Colegio de México.

Hirschman, Albert O.
1981   *Essays in Trespassing: Economics to Politics and Beyond.* Cambridge: Cambridge University Press.

Iribarren Pascal, Fr. Pablo
1987   *Visita pastoral a la zona de Ocosingo.* Typed ms.
1988   *Visita pastoral a la zona de Miramar.* Typed ms.
ISMAM
1990   *Manual práctico del cultivo biológico del café orgánico.* Indígenas de la Sierra Madre de Motozintla, San Isidro Labrador. Motozintla, Chiapas: S.O.S. Werelhandel.
de Janvry, Alain
1981   *The Agrarian Question and Reformism in Latin America.* Baltimore: Johns Hopkins University Press.
de Janvry, Alain, Elisabeth Sadoulet, and Gustavo Gordillo de Anda
1994   NAFTA and Mexico's Corn Producers. Paper presented at the XVIII Latin American Studies Association International Congress, March 10-12, 1994, in Atlanta, Georgia.
Karl, Terry L.
n.d.   *The Paradox of Plenty: Oil Booms and Petro-States.* University of California Press, Berkeley, in press.
Leyva Solano, Xóchitl
1994   Militancia político-religiosa e identidad en la Lacandona. Working paper. San Cristóbal de las Casas: CIESAS Sureste.
Leyva Solano, Xóchitl and Gabriel Ascencio Franco
1993   Apuntes para el estudio de la ganaderización en la Selva Lacandona. *Anuario 1992, Instituto Chiapaneco de Cultura,* pp. 262-284.
Loyola, Luis J.
1988   *Brokerage, Capital Accumulation and Development: Transporters in the Process of Economic and Political Change in Chiapas, Mexico.* Ph.D. Dissertation, Graduate Faculty of Anthropology, City University of New York.
Lustig, Nora
1994   Solidarity as a Strategy of Poverty Alleviation. Pp. 79-96 in *Transforming State-Society Relations in Mexico: The National Solidarity Strategy,* ed. by Wayne A. Cornelius, Ann L. Craig, and Jonathan Fox. La Jolla: Center for U.S.-Mexican Studies, University of California, San Diego.
MacLeod, Murdo J.
1973   *Spanish Central America: A Socioeconomic History, 1520-1720.* Berkeley: University of California Press.
Marion Singer, Marie-Odile
1984   *El movimeinto campesino en Chiapas, 1983.* México, D.F.: Centro de Estudios Históricos del Agrarismo en México.
1989   *Las organizaciones campesinas autónomas: un reto a la producción.* México, D.F.: Instituto Nacional de Antropología e Historia.
1994   Crónica de un desastre evitable. *Asuntos Indígenas* 1:18-20.
Méndez Asensio, Luis, and Antonio Cano Gimeno
1994   *La guerra contra el tiempo: Viaje a la selva alzada.* México, D.F.: Espasa Calpa Mexicana, S.A.
Merryman, John
1969   *The Civil Law Tradition: An Introduction to the Legal Systems of Western Europe and Latin America.* Stanford: Stanford University Press.

Minnesota Advocates for Human Rights
1993   *Civilians at Risk: Military and Police Abuses in the Mexican Countryside.*
        Minneapolis: Minnesota Advocates for Human Rights.

Morales Bermúdez, Jesús
1992   El Congreso Indígena de Chiapas: Un Testimonio. *Anuario 1991, Instituto
        Chiapaneco de Cultura*, pp. 242-370.

Morquecho Escamilla, Gaspar
1992   *Los Indios en un Proceso de Organización: La Organización Indígena de los
        Altos de Chiapas. ORIACH.* San Cristóbal de las Casas: Universidad
        Autónoma de Chiapas.

Nash, June
1993   *Crafts in the World Market: The Impact of International Exchange on Middle
        American Artisans.* Edited by June Nash. Albany: SUNY Press.
1994   Global Integration and Subsistence Insecurity. *American Anthropologist*
        96:7-30.

Nash, June, and Kathleen Sullivan
1992   Return to Porfirismo: The Views from the Southern Frontier. *Cultural
        Survival Quarterly* 16(2):13-17.

Nations, James D.
1984   The Lacandones, Gertrude Blom, and the Selva Lacandona. Pp. 26-41 in
        Gertrude Blom: Bearing Witness, Alex Harris and Margaret Sartor, eds.
        Chapel Hill: University of North Carolina Press.
1994   The Ecology of the Zapatista Revolt. *Cultural Survival Quarterly* 18(1):
        31-33.

Nigh, Ronald B.
1992   La agricultura orgánica y el nuevo movimiento campesino en México.
        Antropológicas, Nueva Epoca 3:39-50.
1994   Zapata Rose in 1994: The Indian Rebellion in Chiapas. *Cultural Survival
        Quarterly* 18(1):9-13.

Nigh, Ronald B. and James D. Nations
1980   Tropical Rainforests. *The Bulletin of the Atomic Scientists* March 1980: 12-19.

Oswald, Ursula, Rafael Rodríguez, and Antonio Flores
1986   *Campesinos protagonistas de su historia. (La coalición de los Ejidos Colectivos
        de los Valles del Yaqui y Mayo: una salida a la cultura de la pobreza).* México,
        D.F.: Universidad Autónoma Metropolitana, Unidad Xochimilco.

Paré, Luisa
1988   *El proletariado agrícola en México: campesinos sin tierra o proletarios agríco-
        las?.* Revised edition. México, D.F: Siglo Veintiuno Editores.

Parra Vázquez, Manuel (compiler)
1989   *El subdesarrollo agrícola en los altos de Chiapas.* Serie Agronomía 18,
        Colección Cuadernos Universitarios. México, D.F.: Universidad
        Autónoma Chapingo.
1993   *Estructura económico y desarrollo campesino en la region Altos de Chiapas.*
        Ph.D. dissertation, Facultad de Economía, UNAM. México, D.F.:
        Universidad Nacional Autónoma de México,

Pérez Castro, Ana Bella
1989   *Entre montañas y cafetales: Luchas agrarias en el norte de Chiapas.* Instituto

de Investigaciones Antropológicas, Serie Antropológica 85. México, D.F.:Universidad Nacional Autónoma de México.

Pick, James B., Edgar W. Butler, and Elizabeth L. Lanzer
1989 *Atlas of Mexico*. Boulder: Westview Press.

Pietri, Rene and Claudio Stern
1985 *Petróleo, agricultura y población en el sureste de México*. El Colegio de México, México, D.F.

Pineda, Luz Olivia
1993 *Caciques Culturales: El case de los maestros bilingues en los Altos de Chiapas*. Puebla: Altres Costa-Amic.

Pohlenz C., Juan
1985 La conformación de la frontera entre México y Guatemala: El caso de Nuevo Huixtán en la selva Chiapaneca. Part I, pp. 23-130 in *La formación histórica de la frontera sur*, by Andrés Fábregas, Juan Pohlenz, Mariano Báez, and Gabriel Macías (eds.). Cuadernos de la casa chata 124. México, D.F.: Centro de Investigaciones y Estudios Superiores en Antropología Social.

Reyes Ramos, María Eugenia
1992 *El reparto de tierras y la política agraria en Chiapas, 1914-1988*. México, D.F.: Universidad Nacional Autónoma de México.

Romero, César
1994 *Marcos: ¿Un profesional de la esperanza?* México, D.F.: Grupo Editorial Planeta.

Rosaldo, Renato
1989 *Culture & Truth: The Remaking of Social Analysis*. Boston: Beacon Press.

Rosenbaum, Brenda
1993 *With Our Heads Bowed: The Dynamics of Gender in a Maya Community*. Albany: SUNY Press.

Rus, Diane
1988 Responding to the Crisis: Changing Economic Roles of Indigenous Women in the Chiapas Highlands. Working paper. San Cristóbal de las Casas: INAREMAC.
1990 La crisis económica y la mujer indígena: El caso de Chamula, Chiapas. Document 038-VIII-90. San Cristóbal de las Casas: INAREMAC.

Rus, Jan
1976 Managing Mexico's Indians: The Historical Context and Consequences of Indigenismo. Manuscript prepared for Department of Anthropology, Harvard University.
1983 Whose Caste War? Indians, Ladinos, and the Chiapas "Caste War" of 1869. Pp. 127-168 in *Spaniards and Indians in Southern Mesoamerica*, Murdo J. MacLeod and Robert Wasserstrom, eds. Lincoln: University of Nebraska Press.
1989 The "Caste War" of 1869 from the Indian's Perspective: A Challenge for Ethnohistory. Pp. 1033-1047 in *Memorias, Coloquio Internacional de Mayistas*, Vol. II. México, D.F.: Universidad Nacional Autónoma de México/Centro de Estudios Mayas.
1994 The "Comunidad Revolucionaria Institucional:" The Subversion of Native Government in Highland Chiapas, 1936-1968. Pp. 265-300 in

Everyday Forms of State Formation: Revolution and the Negotiation of Rule in Modern Mexico, eds. Gilbert M. Joseph and Daniel Nugent. Durham: Duke University Press.

n.d. Contained Revolutions: Indians and the Struggle for Control of Highland Chiapas, 1910-1925. Forthcoming, Mexican Studies/Estudios Mexicanos.

Russell, Philip L.
1994 Mexico under Salinas. Austin: Mexico Resource Center.

Ruz, Mario Humberto
1985 Copanaguastla en un espejo: un pueblo Tzeltal en el virreinato. Tuxtla Gutiérrez: Universidad Autónoma de Chiapas.
1992 Savia India, floración Ladina: Apuntes para una historia de las fincas comitecas (siglos XVIII y XIX). México, D.F.: Consejo Nacional para la Cultura y las Artes.

Sánchez, Pontigo and José Luis Ovalle Muñoz
1986 Lucha laboral y sindicalismo en Simojovel y Huitiupán, Chiapas. Pp. 153-160 in Asalariados agrícolas y sindicalismo en el campo mexicano, ed. by Hubert C. de Grammont. México, D.F.: Joan Pablos Editor, S.A./Instituto de Investigaciones Sociales, UNAM.

Sanderson, Steven E.
1986 The Transformation of Mexican Agriculture: International Structure and the Politics of Rural Change. Princeton: Princeton University Press.

Scherr, Sara J.
1985 The Oil Syndrome and Agricultural Development: Lessons from Tabasco, Mexico. New York: Praeger Publishers.

Silko, Leslie Marmon
1991 Almanac of the Dead: A Novel. New York: Penguin Books USA, Inc.

Spalding, Rose J.
1984 The Mexican Food Crisis: An Analysis of the SAM. Research Report Series, 33. La Jolla: Center for U.S.-Mexican Studies, University of California, San Diego.

Spenser, Daniela
1988 El Partido Socialista Chiapaneco: rescate y reconstrucción de su historia. Ediciones de la Casa Chata 29. México, D.F.: Centro de Investigaciones y Estudios Superiores en Antropología Social.

Stavenhagen, Rodolfo
1975 Social Classes in Agrarian Societies. Translated by J. A. Hellman. Garden City, New York: Anchor Books.

Taller de Análisis de las Cuestiones Agrarias
1988 Los Zapatistas de Chiapas. San Cristóbal de las Casas: Taller de Análisis de las Cuestiones Agrarias.

Taller Tzotzil
1988 Buch'u la smeltzan Jobel?/Quien hizo San Cristóbal. San Cristóbal de las Casas: INAREMAC.
1990 Abtel ta pinka/Trabajo en las fincas. San Cristóbal de las Casas: INAREMAC.

Toledo, Victor M.
1994 La vía ecológico-campesina de desarrollo: Una alternativa para la selva de

Chiapas. *La Jornada del Campo* 2(23):4-6.

Toledo Tello, Sonia
n.d.   *Simojovel: La lucha actual contra la servidumbre agraria.* Unpublished manuscript. San Cristóbal de las Casas: Centro de Estudios Indígenas, Universidad Nacional Autónoma de Chiapas.

Union "Tierra Tzotzil"
1990   *Kipaltik: Lo'il sventa k'u cha'al la jmankutik jpinkakutik/La historia de como compramos nuestra finca.* San Cristóbal de las Casas: INAREMAC (Instituto de Asesoría Antropológica para la Región Maya, A.C.).

Varese, Stefano
1992   Grupos No Gubermentales y Organizaciones de Base. Manuscript, Chapter 8, for *Agricultural Sector Reform and the Peasantry in Mexico,* for Special Programming Mission to Mexico, International Fund for Agricultural Development. Rome: United Nations, July 1992.

Vasconcelos, José
1948   *La raza cósmica: Misión de la raza Iberoamericana, Argentina y Brazil.* México D.F.: Espasa-Calpa Mexicana.

Villafuerte Solís, Daniel (ed.)
1993   *El café en la frontera sur: La producción y los productores del Soconusco, Chiapas.* Tuxtla Gutiérrez: Instituto Chiapaneco de Cultura.

Viqueira Albán, Juan Pedro
1993   *María de la Candelaria: India natural de Cancuc.* México, D.F.: Fondo de Cultura Económica.

Vogt, Evon Z.
1969   *Zinacantan: A Maya Community in the Highlands of Chiapas.* Cambridge: Harvard University Press.

de Vos, Jan
1980   *La paz de Dios y del Rey: La conquista de la Selva Lacandona por los españoles, 1525-1821.* México, D.F.: Gobierno del Estado de Chiapas.

1988   *Oro verde: La conquista de la Selva Lacandona por los madereros tabasqueños, 1822-1949.* México, D.F.: Fondo de Cultura Económica.

Warman, Arturo
1980   *"We Come to Object." The Peasants of Morelos and the National State.* Translated by Stephen K. Ault. Baltimore: The Johns Hopkins University Press.

Wasserstrom, Robert
1983   *Class and Society in Central Chiapas.* Berkeley: University of California Press.

Wilkie, James W.
1970   *The Mexican Revolution: Federal Expenditure and Social Change since 1910.* Berkeley and Los Angeles: University of California Press.

Williams, Robert G.
1986   *Export Agriculture and the Crisis in Central America.* Chapel Hill: University of North Carolina Press.

Wolf, Eric R.
1969   *Peasant Wars of the Twentieth Century.* New York: Harper & Row.

Wolf, Eric R. and Edward C. Hansen
1972   *The Human Condition in Latin America.* New York: Oxford University Press.

Index

About the Authors

George A. Collier obtained a Ph.D. in Social Anthropology from Harvard University. He is Professor of Anthropology, Stanford University, where he has also served as Chair of Anthropology and Director, Center for Latin American Studies. Dr. Collier began his studies of agrarian politics and agrarian change in Chiapas, Mexico, in the 1960s. He is author of *Fields of the Tzotzil: The Ecological Bases of Tradition in Highland Chiapas* (University of Texas Press, 1975); *The Inca and Aztec States: Anthropology and History, 1400–1800* (Academic Press, 1982, co-edited with Renato Rosaldo and John Wirth); *Socialists of Rural Andalusia: Unacknowledged Revolutionaries of the Second Republic* (Stanford University Press, 1987), and numerous journal articles.

Elizabeth Lowery Quaratiello, a graduate of Wheaton College, is a freelance journalist with interests in anthropology, food, and economics. A former crime reporter, she is married and has one child.

Peter Rosset, Ph.D., a leading rural development specialist, is currently the Executive Director of Food First after serving two years as the Director of Stanford University's Regional Center in Chiapas, Mexico.

Institute Publications

Alternatives to the Peace Corps: A Directory of Third World and US Volunteer Opportunities by Becky Buell and Annette Olson. Now in its sixth edition, this guide provides essential information on voluntary service organizations, technical service programs, work brigades, study tours, as well as alternative travel in the Third World and offers options to the Peace Corps as the principle route for people wishing to gain international experience. $6.95

Brave New Third World? Strategies for Survival in the Global Economy by Walden Bello. Can Third World countries finish the next decade as vibrant societies? Or will they be even more firmly in the grip of underdevelopment? The outcome, Bello argues, depends on their ability to adopt a program of democratic development which would place them on equal footing in the global economy. $6.00

Chile's Free-Market Miracle: A Second Look by Joseph Collins and The economic policies behind the boom experienced by Chile in the 1980s under Pinochet, and continuing today, are widely touted as a model for the Third World. The authors take a closer look at the Chilean experience where they encounter the downside of the model: chronic poverty and environmental devastation. $15.95

Circle of Poison: Pesticides and People in a Hungry World by David Weir and Mark Shapiro. In the best investigation style, this popular expose documents the global scandal of corporate and government exportation of pesticides and reveals the threat this poses to consumers and workers throughout the world. $7.95

Dark Victory: The U.S., Structural Adjustment, and Global Poverty by Walden Bello, with Shea Cunningham and Bill Rau. Offers an understanding of why poverty has deepened in many countries, and analyzes the impact of Reagan-Bush economic policies which resulted in a decline of living standards in much of the Third World, but also in the U.S. The challenge for progressives in the 1990's is to articulate a new agenda based on the reality that the people of the South and North share the tragedy of being victims of the same process that serves the interest of a global minority. $12.95

Dragons in Distress: Asia's Miracle Economies in Crisis by Walden Bello and Stephanie Rosenfeld. Economists often refer to South Korea, Taiwan, and Singapore as "miracle economies," and technocrats regard them as models for the rest of the Third World. The authors challenge these established notions and show how, after three decades of rapid growth, these economies are entering a period of crisis. The authors offer policy recommendations for structural change that would break the NIC's unhealthy dependence on Japan and the U.S. and examine both the positive and negative lessons of the NIC experience for the Third World. $12.95

Education for Action: Graduate Studies with a Focus on Social Change by Andrea Freedman and Nooshi Borhan. A guide to progressive graduate programs and educators in agriculture, anthropology, development studies, economics, ethnic studies, history, law, management, peace studies, political science, public health, sociology, urban planning and women's studies. $6.95

Kerala: Radical Reform as Development in an Indian State by R.W. Franke and B.H. Chasin. Analyzes both the achievements and the limitations of the Kerala experience. In the last eighty years, the Indian state of Kerala has undergone an experiment in the use of radical reform as a development strategy that has brought it some of the Third World's highest levels of health, education, and social justice. 1994 revised edition $9.95

Needless Hunger: Voices from a Bangladesh Village by James Boyce and Betsy Hartmann. The Global analysis of Food First is vividly captured here in a single village. The root causes of hunger emerge through the stories of both village landowners and peasants who live at the margin of survival. Now in its sixth printing! $6.95

No Free Lunch: Food and Revolution in Cuba Today by Medea Benjamin, Joseph Collins and Michael Scott. Based on sources not readily available to Western researchers, this examination of Cuba's food and farming system confirms that Cuba is the only Latin American country to have eradicated hunger. $9.95

People and Power in the Pacific: The Struggle for the Post-Cold War Order by Walden Bello. Examines the extent to which events in the Asia-Pacific reflect the so-called new world order; the future role of the U.S. and the emergence of Japan as a key economic power on the world stage. $12.00

The Philippines: Fire on the Rim by Joseph Collins. Looks at the realities following the People Power revolution in the Philippines. A choir of voices from peasants, plantation managers, clergy, farmers, prostitutes who serve U.S. military bases, mercenaries, revolutionaries and others, speak out. *Hardcover* $9.50, *Paper* $5.00.

Taking Population Seriously by Frances Moore Lappé and Rachel Schurman. The authors conclude that high fertility is a response to antidemocratic power structures that leave people with little choice but to have many children. The authors do not see the solution as more repressive population control, but instead argue for education and improved standard of living. $7.95

Trading Freedom: How Free Trade Affects Our Lives, Work, and Environment edited by John Cavanagh, John Gershman, Karen Baker and Gretchen Helmke. Contributors from Mexico, Canada and the U.S. analyze the North American Free Trade Agreement. Drawing on the experiences of communities in Canada, the U.S., and Mexico, this comprehensive collection provides a hard-hitting critique of the current proposals for a continental free trade zone through an intensive examination of its impact on the environment, workers, consumers, and women. $5.00

Curricula

Exploding the Hunger Myths: A High School Curriculum by Sonja Williams. With an emphasis on hunger, twenty-five activities provide a variety of positive discovery experiences—role playing, simulation, interviewing, writing, drawing—to help students understand the real underlying causes of hunger and how problems they thought were inevitable can be changed. 200 pages, 8.5x11 with charts, reproducible illustrated handouts, resource guide and glossary. $15.00

Food First Curriculum by Laurie Rubin. Six delightfully illustrated units span a range of compelling topics including the path of food from farm to table, why people in other parts of the world do things differently, and how young people can help make changes in their communities. 146 pages, three-hole punched, 8.5x11 with worksheets and teacher's resources. $12.00

Food First Comic by Leonard Rifas. An inquisitive teenager sets out to discover the roots of hunger. Her quest is illustrated with wit and imagination by Rifas, who has based his comic on *World Hunger: Twelve Myths*. $1.00

Write or call our distributor to place book orders. All orders must be prepaid. Please add $4.00 for the first book and $1.00 for each additional book for shipping and handling.

Subterranean Company
Box 160, 265 South 5th Street
Monroe, OR 97456
(800) 274-7826

About the Institute

The Institute for Food and Development Policy, publisher of this book, is a nonprofit research and education for action center. The Institute works to identify the root causes of hunger and poverty in the United States and around the world, and to educate the public as well as policymakers about these problems.

The world has never produced so much food as it does today—more than enough to feed every child, woman, and man. Yet hunger is on the rise, with more than one billion people around the world going without enough to eat.

Institute research has demonstrated that the hunger and poverty in which millions seem condemned to live is not inevitable. Our Food First publications reveal how scarcity and overpopulation, long believed to be the causes of hunger, are instead symptoms—symptoms of an ever-increasing concentration of control over food-producing resources in the hands of a few, depriving so many people of the power to feed themselves. In 55 countries and 20 languages, Food First materials and investigations are freeing people from the grip of despair, laying the groundwork—in ideas and action—for a more democratically controlled food system that will meet the needs of all.

An Invitation to Join Us

Private contributions and membership dues form the financial base of the Institute for Food and Development Policy. Because the Institute is not tied to any government, corporation, or university, it can speak with a strong independent voice, free of ideological formulas. The success of the Institute's programs depends not only on its dedicated volunteers and staff, but on financial activists as well. All our efforts toward ending hunger are made possible by membership dues or gifts from individuals, small foundations, and religious organizations. We accept no government or corporate funding.

Each new and continuing member strengthens our effort to change a hungry world. We'd like to invite you to join in this effort. As a member of the Institute you will receive a 25 percent discount on all Food First books. You will also receive our quarterly publication, Food First News and Views, and our timely Action Alerts. The alerts provide information and suggestions for action on current food and hunger crises in the United States and around the world.

All contributions to the Institute are tax deductible.

To join us in putting food first, just clip and return the attached coupon to:

Institute for Food and Development Policy,
398 60th Street, Oakland, CA 94618
(510) 654-4400

Name _____

Address _____

City/State/Zip _____

Daytime Phone ( ) _____

❏ I want to join Food First and receive a 25% discount on this and all subsequent orders. Enclosed is my tax-deductible contribution of:

❏ $100   ❏ $50   ❏ $30

PAGE	ITEM DESCRIPTION	QTY	UNIT COST	TOTAL
T-shirts ❏ XL ❏ L ❏ M ❏ S			$12.00	

Payment Method: ❏ Check   ❏ Money Order   ❏ Mastercard   ❏ Visa

For gift mailings, please see other side of this coupon.

Name on Card _____

Card Number _____Exp. Date _____

Signature _____

Member discount -25%	$ _____
CA Residents 8.5%	$ _____
SUBTOTAL	$ _____
Postage/15%-UPS/20% ($2 min.)	$ _____
Membership(s)	$ _____
Contribution	$ _____
TOTAL ENCLOSED	$ _____

Make check payable to Subterranean Company, Box 160, 265 South 5th St., Monroe, OR 97456

Please send a Gift Membership to:

Name _____

Address _____

City/State/Zip _____

From _____

Please send a Gift Book to:

Name _____

Address _____

City/State/Zip _____

From _____

Please send a Resource Catalog to:

Name _____

Address _____

City/State/Zip _____

Name _____

Address _____

City/State/Zip _____

Name _____

Address _____

City/State/Zip _____

Name _____

Address _____

City/State/Zip _____